Making the Most of

Counselling *and* Psychotherapy Placements

SAGE was founded in 1965 by Sara Miller McCune to support the dissemination of usable knowledge by publishing innovative and high-quality research and teaching content. Today, we publish more than 750 journals, including those of more than 300 learned societies, more than 800 new books per year, and a growing range of library products including archives, data, case studies, reports, conference highlights, and video. SAGE remains majority-owned by our founder, and after Sara's lifetime will become owned by a charitable trust that secures our continued independence.

Los Angeles | London | Washington DC | New Delhi | Singapore

Making the Most of Counselling and Psychotherapy Placements

Michelle Oldale *and* Michelle J. Cooke

Los Angeles | London | New Delhi
Singapore | Washington DC | Boston

Los Angeles | London | New Delhi
Singapore | Washington DC

SAGE Publications Ltd
1 Oliver's Yard
55 City Road
London EC1Y 1SP

SAGE Publications Inc.
2455 Teller Road
Thousand Oaks, California 91320

SAGE Publications India Pvt Ltd
B 1/I 1 Mohan Cooperative Industrial Area
Mathura Road
New Delhi 110 044

SAGE Publications Asia-Pacific Pte Ltd
3 Church Street
#10-04 Samsung Hub
Singapore 049483

Editor: Susannah Trefgarne
Assistant editor: Laura Walmsley
Production editor: Rachel Burrows
Copyeditor: Solveig Gardner Servian
Proofreader: Danielle Ray
Indexer: Martin Hargreaves
Marketing manager: Camille Richmond
Cover design: Shaun Mercier
Typeset by: C&M Digitals (P) Ltd, Chennai, India
Printed and bound by CPI Group (UK) Ltd,
Croydon, CR0 4YY

© Michelle Oldale and Michelle J. Cooke 2015

First published 2015

Apart from any fair dealing for the purposes of research or private study, or criticism or review, as permitted under the Copyright, Designs and Patents Act, 1988, this publication may be reproduced, stored or transmitted in any form, or by any means, only with the prior permission in writing of the publishers, or in the case of reprographic reproduction, in accordance with the terms of licences issued by the Copyright Licensing Agency. Enquiries concerning reproduction outside those terms should be sent to the publishers.

Library of Congress Control Number: 2014950922

British Library Cataloguing in Publication data

A catalogue record for this book is available from the British Library

ISBN 978-1-4462-0845-8
ISBN 978-1-4462-0846-5 (pbk)

At SAGE we take sustainability seriously. Most of our products are printed in the UK using FSC papers and boards. When we print overseas we ensure sustainable papers are used as measured by the Egmont grading system. We undertake an annual audit to monitor our sustainability.

Contents

List of Activities	vi
List of Figures and Tables	vii
About the Authors	viii
Acknowledgements	ix
Introduction	x

1	Defining placement: historical background and context	1
2	Preparing for placement: personal, theoretical and ethical considerations	24
3	Before you start: training provider and wider professional considerations	51
4	The placement search, application and interview process	82
5	Commencing placement: managing practicalities, processes and relationships	113
6	Placements in perspective	144

Index	165

List of Activities

1.1	Exploring initial responses to the idea of placement	2
1.2	Historical treatment of mental distress, implications in placement	10
1.3	Exploring organisational experience	19
1.4	Exploring placement contexts	20
2.1	Consideration of motivations to practise	27
2.2	Considering philosophical and theoretical understanding	34
2.3	Reflections on 'ethics' in preparation for placement	36
2.4	Ethical considerations in the readiness to practise assessment process	38
2.5	Considering personal development and readiness to practise	40
2.6	Reflection on professional development	42
2.7	Pre-placement practical considerations	46
3.1	Training provider assessment of readiness	55
3.2	Responses to being assessed	59
4.1	Evaluating placements and deciding where to apply	91
4.2	Preparing a personal statement	94
4.3	Possible interview questions	103
4.4	Reflecting on feedback	109
5.1	Familiarising yourself with the placement organisation	114
5.2	Beginning placement – approaches to planning	116
5.3	Assumptions about the client	129
5.4	Exploring the possible impact of the first session	134
5.5	Ways of utilising session material for professional development; practical and ethical considerations	140
6.1	Applying appreciative questions to aspects of practice	146
6.2	Personal reflections on ending with a placement	152

List of Figures and Tables

Figures

1.1	Placement influences	14
2.1	The decision-making process	30
2.2	Factors accounting for change in therapy	34
3.1	Responding to feedback	65
3.2	Function of supervision	72
4.1	Example curriculum vitae – placements	97
5.1	The therapeutic process	126
6.1	Function of supervision	161

Tables

1.1	Contextualising placement in training and qualification	5
1.2	Exploring placement contexts grid	21
2.1	Reflection on professional development	43
2.2	Reflections on ethics – weekly schedule	47
3.1	Assessment of readiness grid	56
3.2	Responses to being assessed	60
3.3	Observed readiness to practise session example feedback form	63
3.4	Three- and four-handed contracts	76
4.1	Placement search and application preparation sheet	84
4.2	Placement search record form	90
4.3	Preparing a personal statement	95
4.4	Possible interview questions	104
4.5	Errors in thinking	107
4.6	Reflecting on feedback grid	110
5.1	Beginning placement – approaches to planning 1	117
5.2	Beginning placement – approaches to planning 2	118
5.3	Induction considerations	120
6.1	Applying appreciative questions to aspects of practice	147
6.2	Appreciative questions on key areas of experience	149
6.3	Continuing professional development activity log	159

About the Authors

Michelle Oldale is a UKCP registered psychotherapist. She is a supervisor and trainer with experience in Further and Higher Education settings most recently with the Sherwood Psychotherapy Training Institute and the Open University. Her interests lie in D/deafness, and disability and the activities of counselling and psychotherapy, training and research. She is a keen writer and regularly reviews books for *Healthcare Counselling and Psychotherapy Journal*. Michelle lives with her family in Nottingham, and when she is not working enjoys singing, CrossFit, arts and crafts and travelling.

Michelle Cooke has worked within a variety of therapeutic settings and maintains a private practice providing psychotherapy and supervision to individuals, couples and groups. She is a UKCP registered psychotherapist. In addition, Michelle works as both Programme Leader and trainer at the Sherwood Psychotherapy Training Institute in Nottingham. Her interests include the evolution of person-centred theory in light of ever-changing thinking within the therapeutic world and beyond. In addition, she is specifically interested in diversity issues relating to the processes of self-criticism, gender and social change.

Acknowledgements

We would like to thank all of those who have been supportive as this book was conceived and came into fruition. It has been a long journey! We offer our heartfelt gratitude to the editors and staff at SAGE for their patience and encouragement as we grappled with the demands of being first-time book authors alongside our full-time roles, as well as everything else life had to throw at us. Finally, we would like to thank those who generously shared their placement-related experience as participants in the research that contributed to this endeavour.

Michelle Oldale: Thank you to Shaun for your unwavering solidity, and to Libby for the occasional prod and Post-it Note. To Michelle Cooke, thank you for believing in the idea and staying the distance!

Michelle Cooke: First, thank you to Michelle Oldale for your trust and loving support during the process of completing this project; this has contributed to sustaining my levels of dedication and determination in the face of a variety of obstacles. Also, I extend my gratitude to my daughter for convincing me that writing could become a key aspect of my calling and career in psychotherapy.

Introduction

Why did we write this book?

This book was conceived as a result of the authors' experiences initially as trainees and latterly as trainers facilitating counselling and psychotherapy trainees to navigate the complexities inherent within the processes of searching for, securing and undertaking a placement. On deciding to undertake a search for a resource for recommendation to trainees embarking on the early stages of the placement process, we were astonished to find that despite there being a wealth of texts for business students, nurses, social workers and teachers, no book existed specifically tailored to meet the needs of those training within the counselling and psychotherapy profession. Although we had developed resources for use within the training context, we thought it would be useful to reach a wider audience; for all those involved in the placement process to have access to a resource which could potentially support and guide them through the important decisions necessary at each stage of the process with the view to supporting self-reflection and prompting consideration of philosophy, theory and practice. Thus, a conversation with SAGE Publications commenced, and the result is the book you are now holding.

We hope that this book supports the view that placements represent more for trainees than a simple accumulation of hours with clients. We have intentionally framed placements as a wider professional and personal endeavour which will influence future development and opportunities, including the potential employability of a therapist. In this way we hope that the experience can be as rewarding as possible for all of the stakeholders concerned. Our vision is to reflect and promote ethical practice based in the uniqueness of the four-way relationship between trainee, training provider, placement provider and supervisor (as well as the wider profession and other frameworks such as the law), whilst acknowledging that the key stakeholder in the process of the placement is the client or service user – an assumption we have made throughout. Thus, we hope that a firm foundation can be built for practice in placement, and that any potential pitfalls can be worked through within this contextualised and relational support structure.

How did we write this book?

At each stage of the process we have attempted to take a relational stance illustrating the collaborative relationships involved within placement provision. We hope that this text reflects the importance of these interconnections between trainee, placement provider, training organisation and supervisor in terms of support for the trainee. Furthermore, it is our intention that this text highlights how the requirements and responsibilities of each party in the network can be fulfilled effectively. In order to achieve this, we have tried to step into the shoes of each to consider what they might gain from reading and using this book.

Who is this book for?

This book is intended primarily for trainee counsellors and psychotherapists. However, we have anticipated that the audience may be wider and may include trainers, supervisors and placement providers themselves. We hope that trainers will be inspired to use and/or adapt activities to suit the specifics of their training content when considering placement provision. Equally, we hope that the book will provide useful insight into some of the practices sometimes taken for granted as 'givens' within the training and placement processes. We anticipate this will benefit both the trainee and those individuals involved in placement provision.

Key terms

Psychotherapist/counsellor

We are aware of the ongoing debates in regard to defining these terms, including attempts to clarify distinctions between them to protect the terms as part of the discussion about statutory regulation of the profession. It is outside the scope of this text to explore these debates in any detail. However, interested readers may find a synopsis of the arguments in Bond (2010: 30–2). Throughout the text we refer to the terms 'psychotherapist' and 'counsellor', we also make use of the term 'therapist' to mean either counsellor or psychotherapist. Our rationale for using the terms synonymously, as well as use of the word 'therapist', is founded upon the fact that the core of psychotherapy and counselling trainings remain broadly constant, that is:

- therapeutic skills and attitudes
- theory
- ethics
- personal/professional development, including placement and other clinical components.

We use the term 'trainee' therapist throughout when referring to those undertaking counselling and psychotherapy training. In this way we hope to acknowledge the activity of training as a professional endeavour from the outset.

Competence versus fitness

Throughout the text you will see us refer to the terms 'competence' and 'fitness' and it is worth highlighting at the outset the difference between these ideas. The British Association for Counselling and Psychotherapy (BACP) (2012: 16) define **competence** as 'to be able to do something'. Competence refers to the concrete skills, qualities and knowledge (e.g. ethical and theoretical) which can be assessed in a discrete way. Just because we *can* do something, however, it does not mean that we *should*. **Fitness** to practise includes a plethora of other factors, such as our wellbeing and personal circumstances. Competence can be said to be a component of fitness but it is not the whole story. When assessing fitness to practise, we take into account a broad range of life circumstances to determine whether it is ethical to be seeing clients at a particular time. For example, a therapist who has recently suffered a bereavement or trauma would use the support mechanisms available to them (e.g. their supervisor and close colleagues) to make a personal assessment of their fitness to practise during this time. The outcome will depend very much on the individual situation and may include ceasing practice for a while, reducing caseload or regulating the types of clients seen for a period of time, increasing supervisory support or attending personal therapy.

You will notice, then, throughout this book that some sections and activities focus on the development of your competence, some on assessment of your fitness. We hope that you will engage with these in collaboration with those who support you in order to come to an evaluation of your personal and professional needs in respect of each.

How to use this book

There may be some for whom this book will be applicable from beginning to end and as such it will represent a companion throughout the entirety of your placement process (or even before you embark on professional training). Equally, some readers are likely to be currently engaged in the placement process either as volunteers, managers, trainers or supervisors and, consequently, will be accessing this text for a variety of different reasons. As such, and to ensure that maximum benefit is gained by a wide range of readers, we have structured each chapter in the following manner:

- **Chapter objectives** provide a snapshot of what you can expect, enabling quick identification of what will be of use to you within the specific chapter.
- **An introductory section** expands on this, giving further detail.
- The main body of the chapter uses **illustrations** and **activities** which can be used by the individual trainee, trainer, supervisor or placement provider in various circumstances. Each activity includes a specific aim (or a set of aims), relevant background taken from the main body of the text and clear instructions about how to engage with the activity itself. For trainees you may wish to think about how your responses to activities will form a bank of useful material for personal and professional reflection. You may also wish to think about when it might be appropriate to revisit activities at different stages in your training and future career.

We acknowledge that trainers may wish to use our activities and therefore we have presented them as worksheets so that they may be used in a training and/or supervisory context.

- **Side notes** have been devised for trainee readers who will be accessing this text at different points in their training journey. It may be that some have bought this book in order to familiarise themselves with the overall requirements of a counselling or psychotherapy training. Some readers may be partway through their training and have purchased this text as part of their preparation for the placement search and application. For this reason we have attempted to avoid assumptions about prior knowledge and have offered definition of terms where applicable in side notes to the main text. You can see an example of a side note on this page.

> **A note about safety.** We, of course, hope that activities throughout the text will be useful to your development as a therapist. When undertaking activities please be mindful of your own self-care and the emotional safety of those who may be undertaking activities with you. This is key in particular when you are undertaking activities alone rather than, for instance, in a training or supervisory context, and when you are asked to reflect on your own development and personal material. You may wish to consider now who might support you in the event that you encounter difficulty so that the support network is in place from the outset.

- At various points we have included **vignettes** which have the function of:
  - illustrating key points
  - critiquing the authors' perspective and offering potential alternatives
  - challenging 'accepted wisdom' and norms within the profession in the spirit of open dialogue
  - highlighting possible discrepancies between the ideal and the practical which in reality is likely to result in compromise.

  Although the vignettes are fictional creations of the authors, we must thank the various individuals and organisations who have supported us in gathering information on which to base these. We hope that the voices reflect a variety of perspectives of the various stakeholders involved in the placement endeavour.

- **The chapter summary** draws together themes and invites further reflection in an **ongoing reflections** section. Reflections are based broadly on Kolb's (1984) learning cycle:
  - Concrete experience – the reading of the chapter and engagement with activities.
  - Reflective observation – capturing key learning points and reflection in regard to activities.
  - Abstract conceptualisation – concluding your learning from the experience and making points for action.
  - Active experimentation – setting goals, objectives and timeframes for any further action or learning you wish to undertake.

  This process is cyclical (once active experimentation is complete we return to the concrete experience stage). We recognise that this process is ongoing and that trainees may wish to revisit reflective activities at different times in the placement process.

- The chapter concludes with **references** and suggestions for **further reading**.

Recording your progress and learning

Most institutions offering counselling and psychotherapy training will encourage trainees to use a training journal, or similar, to enable trainees to capture key learning points as they occur. You may wish to use your journal if you have one already, or start a specific journal in which to record responses to activities, ongoing reflections invited at the end of each chapter, and any other points of interest which arise.

Final thoughts

We would like to stress that we welcome feedback from professionals working in all aspects of the placement process. In the event that a second edition of this book will follow, any feedback will enable us to develop the text in the light of changes in the field and your comments. As we invite trainees to develop reflexive practice we hope that our own embracing of this approach will lead to continuous improvement of a text which has long been missing from the field, as well as supporting our own development as therapists, trainers, supervisors and authors.

References

Bond, T. (2010) *Standards and Ethics for Counselling in Action*, 3rd edn. London: Sage.
British Association for Counselling and Psychotherapy (BACP) (2012) *Accreditation of Training Courses*. Lutterworth: British Association for Counselling and Psychotherapy.
Kolb, D.A. (1984) *Experiential Learning: Experience as the Source of Learning and Development*. Upper Saddle River, NJ: Prentice Hall.

One
Defining Placement: Historical Background and Context

This chapter will:

- Introduce the concept of placement within the professional fields of counselling and psychotherapy.
- Explore origins and definitions of the term, including consideration of the historical context in regard to counselling and psychotherapy and potential implications for contemporary placement practice.
- Consider the significance of placements for the stakeholders involved: the trainee, training organisation, placement provider and wider profession of counselling and psychotherapy.
- Highlight the nature of the placement including the influence of individual, organisational and socio-political factors.
- Present an overview of some of the contexts in which placements are offered and practised.

Within the United Kingdom, the term 'placement' is widely used by both training providers and associated professional bodies specialising in counselling and psychotherapy. Typically this term refers to specific work-based requirements including, but not limited to, the undertaking of supervised client work. Placement-based experience such as this is thought to bridge the gap between practice undertaken with colleagues in the training context and a possible lifelong career within the field. According to Mearns (1997), the term 'placement' has been adopted from the tradition of social work training in which it refers to students being 'placed' into a practice context by their training organisation, with the primary purpose of securing relevant work-based experience prior to qualification.

Although undertaking a placement is accepted as being among the first steps in the trainee therapist's journey towards gaining the experience deemed essential to securing recognised professional status, there are some clear differences in definition and the nature of the endeavour when comparing to professions such as social work. Equally, for those who are new to counselling and psychotherapy training or those transitioning from careers outside of the health and social care professions, the idea of undertaking what is normally an unpaid position in order to gain extensive pre-qualification experience may seem somewhat unusual.

In order to explore these ideas further, this chapter examines the concept of placement, offering definition and consideration of its nature within the professional fields of counselling and psychotherapy. The implications for contemporary practice are addressed in light of historical and cultural perspectives inherent within the profession. In this chapter we outline the main types of experience and learning you may be asked to secure as a trainee and examine the significance of the placement for each of its stakeholders. Several placement settings are considered in order to provide some concrete examples of the nature of the placement experience and to illustrate the influence of individual, organisational and socio-political factors. Further reading in each of the key areas is outlined, and you will find a range of activities incorporated to assist you to explore personal responses to the ideas presented. Before you start to read the rest of the chapter, you may wish to undertake Activity 1.1 which offers an opportunity for you to record your initial thoughts and feelings about finding a placement. You might reflect on the things you have noted as you read through the chapter, highlighting those that have been reinforced, challenged or changed.

Activity 1.1 Exploring initial responses to the idea of placement

Aim

- To facilitate exploration of initial responses to the prospect of undertaking a counselling/psychotherapy placement.

Background

A placement is the work-based experience where the trainee will gain their vocational or 'on the job' experience. For the counselling and psychotherapy trainee this usually means taking on an unpaid role in:

- an organisation offering therapeutic services as a primary function
- an organisation offering therapeutic support as a secondary or pastoral service to staff or service users.

Activity

Take a few moments to reflect upon sensations … feelings … thoughts … any images which arise for you as you consider the idea of a placement. Make note of these in any way you wish, be these words, images or any other means.

A PDF version of this activity is available to download from https://study.sagepub.com/oldaleandcooke

What is a placement?

Put simply, the term 'placement' refers to the work-based undertaking in which the trainee in counselling and/or psychotherapy gains their vocational or 'on the job' learning experience. This usually means taking on an unpaid role in:

- an organisation offering therapeutic services as a primary function in the form of a dedicated counselling or psychotherapy service
- an organisation offering therapeutic services as a secondary or pastoral service to staff or service users. For example, working in an educational setting, general practice (GP) surgery or as part of a workplace counselling service.

In much the same way as a social worker, nurse, doctor or teacher gains experience prior to qualification and securing a paid role in their profession, trainee counsellors and psychotherapists also work towards gaining professional experience in this way. However, there is a key distinction between the nature of the counselling and psychotherapy placement and those undertaken within other helping professions. Whilst the trainee social worker, nurse, teacher or doctor is able to be accompanied and directly supervised by a more senior colleague in their initial face-to-face interactions with service users, this is not generally the case for those training in order to enter the profession of counselling and psychotherapy. The stereotypical image of the qualified doctor on their hospital ward rounds followed closely by a group of medical students is an atypical scenario in the counselling and psychotherapy world. Counselling and psychotherapy is fundamentally an encounter which takes place privately between therapist and client; there tends to be no direct third party involvement within the encounter.

This means that from the outset many trainee therapists work directly and unaccompanied with clients. There are, of course,

> Volunteering England (www.volunteering.org.uk) defines volunteering as 'any activity that involves spending time, unpaid, doing something that aims to benefit the environment or someone (individuals or groups) other than, or in addition to, close relatives'. They stress that the choice to do this is autonomously made by the individual. In this way a trainee therapist might see themselves as a volunteer despite the fact that their placement is a requirement of gaining their qualification and professional status. Trainees may also find that some placement organisations expect a commitment to undertaking tasks over and above counselling; for example, administrative duties in the spirit of gaining a wider knowledge and integration into the organisation as a whole.

> Observations may be more common in psychological settings where this as well as co-working may take place as part of the training process. Contexts offering couples or family therapy may also support observation or collaborative working to support the development of the trainee practitioner. Occasionally two-way mirrors may be used to facilitate observation with minimal intrusion on the session.

exceptions to this; for example, in situations where co-therapists or interpreters are part of the process.

Having undertaken my nurse training, the idea of placement is not new to me; however, thinking about what this means in a different professional context initially raised some anxiety as the expectations seemed very different. Working unaccompanied with a client was a far cry from being surrounded by peers and more experienced colleagues on the ward to whom I could immediately ask questions or raise concerns. Talking about this in training helped me to realise that others shared my concerns and that I did not have to come up with the perfect response every time or know everything on the spot. Asking for time to reflect on a question that a client might ask is a perfectly reasonable thing to do and this allows time to get the professional support needed to make an appropriate and ethical response, gaining the support of those in the placement and my supervisor, even though they are not there in the room with me at the time.

The role and purpose of the placement in counselling and psychotherapy

Contemporary counselling and psychotherapy training providers widely accept that some closely supervised, pre-qualification experience is an essential component in the process of becoming recognised within this professional field. Those undertaking training may not necessarily have experience in the field of professional helping, so their initial experience of the 'helping' and/or therapy role will likely be within the training context, with the first 'actual client' being seen within the placement setting. As discussed previously, the majority of counselling and psychotherapy placements tend to be undertaken in a voluntary or unpaid capacity. Placement opportunities are available in a wide variety of contexts (some of which are outlined later in this chapter), and many training providers require trainees to gain experience in more than one setting.

It is generally the responsibility of the trainee therapist to search for an appropriate placement opportunity (see Chapter 4). We see each stakeholder in the process as holding unique responsibilities and these are usually outlined in three- and four-handed contracts (see Chapter 3). Although there is some overlap, the responsibilities of the various parties are likely to include:

- **Training provider** – Structured delivery of training designed to develop trainee competence and fitness to practise as a therapist. Generally this will involve input on psychotherapeutic/counselling theory, ethics/professional development, therapeutic skills and personal development.
- **Placement provider** – Provision of therapeutic services and allocation of clients with whom therapists may gain concrete experience. Other benefits may be offered to the trainee (e.g. supervision, further client group specific training) dependent upon the size and nature of the organisation.

- **Supervisor** – Provision of time and space for reflection on practice to support the professional development of the therapist (further definition is provided in Chapter 3).
- **Trainee** – Engage with training, placement and supervision (e.g. in a way which ensures ongoing competence and fitness to practise in line with all stakeholder ethical and professional requirements).

Types of placement experience

Consideration of a cross-section of UK-based training providers suggests there are three key types of placement experience and learning you may be expected to undertake as you work towards gaining a qualification and professional recognition. Table 1.1 presents a summary of the nature of each.

TABLE 1.1 *Contextualising placement in training and qualification*

Placements integrated within a programme of study/recognised qualification	
Work-based learning, for example: • administrative tasks • attending meetings • wider training	Supervised client work
Shorter module-based placements	
For example, observational experience in order to understand particular roles within mental health and their interface with counselling or psychotherapy.	
Post-qualification placements	
Designed to accrue sufficient work-based experience and learning, including supervised client hours to enable application for accreditation or registration.	

What the trainee does in placement, the nature of the experience and the learning that derives from that experience will vary enormously according to the specific type of placement being undertaken (see Table 1.1) as well as context-specific factors (e.g. policy and procedure within the organisation; client group; environment; supervisor input). What the trainee gains from the experience will also vary according to their engagement with the learning and development opportunities provided by the different stakeholders mentioned in the previous section. The professional development of the therapist is a primary aim and the placement environment is expected to support this by offering opportunities to develop competencies, capabilities and attitudes consistent with practice in the field. Both professional bodies and training institutions take an active involvement in defining the expectations of a placement and, like each of the other stakeholders mentioned above, have a vested interest in the quality of placement processes. These interests are outlined in the forthcoming sections with the aim of grounding and contextualising the meaning of the activity for each.

Significance for the trainee

For the trainee in counselling and psychotherapy there is always the problematic question of 'Where do I start?'. Whilst practising with colleagues within the training group is usually a first experience, at some point, whether you have prior experience or not, it is necessary to see clients in the 'real world' to build clinical competence in terms of skills and attitudes and the application of theoretical and ethical knowledge gained in training. This is where placements provide a stepping stone between the training environment and practising more independently as experience builds and qualification is gained. The placement provides an opportunity for the trainee to practise within the security and support of an established organisation. It provides a context in which trainee therapists can work with clients who are (usually) pre-assessed and matched to individual levels of training and experience. This would enable the trainee to safely and ethically build an initial caseload in line with their developing clinical competency. It is important to note that the experience gained in placement is not necessarily limited to the therapeutic endeavour itself. Much can be learned through participating in related activities, such as the administration and management required to support practice. The rewards and complexities of working in a multi-disciplinary environment can be learned in a placement setting which works in this way.

For many trainees the placement will mark the first step into the world of therapy. In this case it is a chance for the trainee to ensure that work as a counsellor or psychotherapist meets their expectations and is a suitable career choice. If it does not, the experience provides a convenient opportunity to reassess and take whatever is needed from the experience thus far. Not everyone who starts training as a counsellor or psychotherapist will end up practising. For those who do, the placement will be a defining learning process and influential to their continuing career development. You will find activities in the next chapter to support you in looking at your motivations to practise and personal readiness.

Significance for the training organisation

Counselling and psychotherapy training providers can be seen as gatekeepers to the profession. Whilst the training context provides some opportunity for assessment of personal and professional development and competence in line with the standards of relevant professional bodies, it is impossible to obtain a fully comprehensive picture as time spent in training passes all too quickly, however well it is managed. Since few training providers have parallel counselling and psychotherapy services attached to them, this normally necessitates the outsourcing of some practice aspects of training to another appropriate context. This enables the training provider to assess via placement provider, supervisor and trainee feedback how trainees are impacted by work with clients and to monitor their continuing personal and professional development in this particular context. In this way the placement provider has an important function in supplementing the assessment role of the training organisation.

Significance for the placement provider

As we will see later in the chapter, placement providers are diverse in the nature of the services they deliver. This diversity means that the significance of taking on counselling and psychotherapy trainees is different for each. Broadly speaking, many services, particularly in the voluntary sector, rely upon the support of an unpaid workforce to provide their particular service. Even where the main workforce are paid employees, calling upon the services of volunteers facilitates a larger and more diverse team meaning there is potentially wider choice for those accessing the service. All of this means that where services apply for renewal of funding or contracts, they have a wider bank of statistical evidence for their efficacy. It could be argued that by maintaining a balance of levels of experience, the fresh enthusiasm of the new trainee can complement the contributions made by those more established in the organisation.

Significance for the profession

The two main professional bodies in counselling and psychotherapy were established relatively recently in view of the historical development of the profession as a whole. The British Association for Counselling (BAC) came into being in 1977 and in 2000 expanded to include membership of psychotherapists (BACP; www.bacp.co.uk/). The United Kingdom Council for Psychotherapy (UKCP; www.ukcp.org.uk/) was set up in 1993. Both bodies set benchmarks and standards of training and professional practice for individual and organisational members, therefore the provision of clinical experience within placement is central to the development of competence for potential future accredited and registered members of these bodies.

Through their activities professional bodies support the development of counselling and psychotherapy. For example, research into what is effective for clients is supported through funding, expertise, and promotion and dissemination of findings through publications and activities and events such as conferences. Ethical codes and frameworks act to support both the therapist and client, meaning that both the service user and the trainee working in placement are supported and protected.

> **UKCP and BACP** are the main professional bodies for psychotherapy and counselling in the United Kingdom. More information is available from:
> - www.psychotherapy.org.uk
> - www.bacp.co.uk

Return now to your reflections gathered during Activity 1.1. Are any of your responses altered now that you have further information about the nature of counselling and psychotherapy placement and the roles and responsibilities of the various stakeholders involved?

The next section gives background on the wider historical and cultural origins of the counselling and psychotherapy profession as a whole. We hope that this will support recognition of how these factors influence contemporary theory and practice – an endeavour which McLeod (2009) sees as vitally important.

Historical background

The counselling and psychotherapy profession, including the placement context, is imbued with residual images, metaphors, expectations and ideas from its past. Consequently, this section highlights some of the key historical and cultural factors likely to have implications for developing your knowledge and understanding of the placement in the context of counselling and psychotherapy training. We include brief consideration of themes evident prior to and including the eighteenth century, followed by an overview of some of the significant influences of the past 200 years. For those of you with a keen interest in developing your historical knowledge and understanding we have listed suggested further reading at the end of the chapter.

The historical 'treatment of distress'

All societies, regardless of geographical location or historical period, have found their own ways to bring about relief to 'sufferers' of emotional and psychological distress and behavioural problems (Dryden and Mytton, 1999). What is deemed 'valid, relevant or effective' has varied according to several factors including the prominent cultural ideology of the time. Most early ideas are thought to have focused on supernatural causes, including possession by the devil or evil spirits. Treatments included administering herbs and ointments, focus on diet, exorcism and mechanical extraction of the 'spirit' thought to be residing within the individual. The early history of medicine indicates a shift in focus, with supernatural explanations being rejected as the cause of emotional or psychological suffering; for example, by Hippocrates in the fifth century BC (Bynum, 2008). In contrast Hippocrates believed that 'mental problems' were caused by 'disequilibrium' within the body, namely the balance between the body's four fluids or humours (blood, yellow bile, black bile and phlegm). Cures lay in removing the humour that was in excess.

Along with the decline of early civilisations and the beginning of the so-called Dark Ages, there was a resurgence of belief in demonic possession and other supernatural causes. Issues of emotional and psychological distress were managed by churches and monasteries. Treatments included prayer, confession, various herbs and potions, being touched by 'relics', and the use of fire and/or water as a means of purification or driving out demons. Historical documentation reports a further shift in the provision of care for the 'insane', with the state assuming control during the thirteen century onwards (Dryden and Mytton, 1999; Porter, 2003). Emphasis on management and control, whether by church or state, did not preclude input by the layperson. Community-based healers remained prominent throughout early history, a practice which continues to date (Rogers and Pilgrim, 2010). Like counselling and psychotherapy, the above explanations and methods involved what might be termed a 'healing relationship' in which one person was thought to need help from another who specialised in understanding and ministering 'treatment', whether this be a 'shaman' (Doniger and Eliage, 2004) or 'physician' (Bynum, 2008) who was sought to 'cure' the afflicted.

Shorter (1997) suggests distinctions between urban and rural responses to care – with the family, as opposed to community, seen as custodian of care within the rural context – whereas, from the Middle Ages onwards, urban solutions for dealing with the 'insane' favoured incarceration (e.g. within an early asylum). Change in social structure brought about by the Industrial Revolution and the Victorian era impacted upon the provision of care. Many people moved from rural communities to settle around areas of industry and employment. These changes in social and economic life were accompanied by shifts in the ways in which family relationships functioned and how emotional and psychological needs were defined and met (McLeod, 2009). During this point in history we see rapid growth in state provision; for example, expansion of the asylum movement from the mid-eighteenth century (Shorter, 1997). It could be argued that much of the current stigma around mental distress has its roots in the barbaric treatment and public ridicule often employed in this era. In contrast, some accounts of this historical period point to the development of more humanitarian perspectives to treatment which respected the suffering of humanity (Dryden and Mytton, 1999).

The eighteenth and nineteenth centuries saw further developments in explanations and treatments, with scientific approaches beginning to take precedence over religious or supernatural viewpoints (Porter, 2003). Major discoveries in the science of electricity were enthusiastically incorporated into the treatment of those incarcerated within asylums, as British asylum doctors sought to establish their professional credentials and claim to be the rightful agents of care of the mentally ill (Beveridge and Renvoize, 1988). A text outlining early notions of symptom clusters or classification of mental disorder was published by Emil Kraepelin (1883, in Dryden and Mytton, 1999). By the early twentieth century, the view that mental illness had at its root a physical cause had gained in popularity and the medical specialism of psychiatry emerged to take its place alongside other areas of medicine. Psychopharmacological and surgical treatments were developed and British psychiatrists regained some interest in the use of electrical methods, introducing electroconvulsive therapy in the late 1930s.

Drawing links to contemporary perspectives, those involved in the provision of therapy today are likely to encounter the influence of these differing historical and cultural positions. For instance, trainees may encounter clients who have experienced

> Psychopharmacology: the treatment of psychological conditions and mental distress with drugs.

shame, ridicule or attack as a result of the prejudice and stigma surrounding their mental illness, whereas others may be fortunate to have been treated humanely regardless of their emotional and psychological state. Furthermore, trainees may find elements of their work impacted by a client's use of a particular medication, and they may hear accounts of other more invasive methods. Activity 1.2 gives the opportunity for reflection on how your placement experience might be influenced by historical and social conceptions of mental distress, and subsequent treatment of those experiencing it.

> ## Activity 1.2 Historical treatment of mental distress, implications in placement
>
> ### Aim
>
> - To facilitate consideration in regard to the potential impact of historical and contemporary views of the 'treatment' of mental distress on placement provision/experience.
>
> ### Background
>
> McLeod (2009: 42) suggests five possible ways in which an appreciation of the history of therapy has meaning and value for present-day practitioners:
>
> 1. Understanding the images of counselling held by members of the public and circulating within contemporary culture.
> 2. Making sense of the underlying metaphors that inform current theories of psychotherapy.
> 3. Reinforcing the sense that counselling represents a continuing tradition that reflects a distinctive set of values and practices.
> 4. Accepting that contemporary ideas and knowledge are incomplete in the absence of a historical perspective.
> 5. A reminder of the significance of power relationships in counselling practice.
>
> ### Activity
>
> With this in mind, what do you think might be the implications of the following for placement provision/experiences?
>
> - Contemporary media images and stereotypical views related to mental health and its treatment.
> - Metaphors that inform current theories of psychotherapy.
> - The idea that counselling is a continuing tradition that reflects a distinctive set of values and practices.
> - The notion that contemporary knowledge is incomplete in the absence of a historical perspective.
> - The significance of power relationships in counselling practice.
>
> *A PDF version of this activity is available to download from https://study.sagepub.com/oldaleandcooke*

I was impacted profoundly by learning about the historical treatment of people suffering from mental ill health when I undertook a counselling skills course. In my ongoing training I decided to seek a placement with an organisation active in fighting the continuing stigma that remains. It feels vitally important to me to mitigate against the ongoing damage caused by these stereotypes. Stories of the impact of this are still told all too frequently by my clients. This saddens me deeply.

My placement is with clients in later life. I am working with a person at the moment who still remembers their mother being taken away to an asylum after the birth of a younger sibling. The sense of loss and injustice they convey is hugely moving, particularly considering that mum was probably suffering from what we might now call post-natal depression.

Counselling and psychotherapy placements – is there a difference?

All of the placements that I have seen say they offer counselling services, and my training course is in psychotherapy. Does this mean that I can't apply to these placements?

Counselling and psychotherapy are two separate yet closely linked traditions. The shifts in society we described in earlier sections laid the groundwork for the emergence of these traditions. Psychotherapy has been described as evolving from the practice of psychiatry, which was the dominant treatment for mental distress at the end of the nineteenth century (Shorter, 1997). The term 'counselling' was first used in the 1940s by Carl Rogers, who lacked the medical training required to adopt the title of psychotherapist (Rogers, 1942). A synopsis of the arguments pertaining to the similarities and differences between the professions can be found in Bond (2010: 30–2), and for those interested in learning more about the emergence of 'counselling' within the United Kingdom we suggest McLeod (2009: 37– 41). What is important for you as a trainee is that the professions of counselling and psychotherapy and their associated trainings tend to be similar in taught content (albeit that academic levels and course length may differ), the implications being that in most instances a trainee can apply for and gain a placement in an organisation offering either counselling and/or psychotherapy.

Different schools of thought

The world of counselling and psychotherapy is made up of numerous perspectives, each with a particular set of ideas about human nature and interaction. Each of us will have developed our own ideas about this, and it is likely that this will influence choice of training. Equally, placement providers may work from particular assumptions about the above, and as such may offer placements to trainees from one particular theoretical perspective or to trainees from a variety of modalities. As you undertake your search you may recognise characteristics of the theoretical ideas below in the organisational practices of the placements you learn about. Unless a placement is specific about the theoretical orientation of therapists recruited, it is likely you will be working with colleagues representing a range of these ideas. As such working relationships can be enhanced by gaining and maintaining a working knowledge of the main approaches practised, and others as you come across them.

From the early 1900s onwards, Freud started his work with 'patients' and formulated his psychoanalytic approach, the 'first force in psychology'. Freud is now popularly known as the 'Father of the Talking Therapies'. Soon afterwards pioneers like Watson, Skinner and Pavlov were making links between animal and human behaviour and conducting experiments into how they could be conditioned towards certain behavioural responses. This marked the rise of the behaviourist approach, or the 'second force'. Beck and Ellis later developed this, combining ideas from cognitive psychology to devise the forerunners of cognitive behavioural therapy (CBT). From the 1940s onwards, humanistic psychology emerged as a number of individual psychologists, such as Maslow, Rogers and Perls, laid the foundations of an alternative to the prevailing 'first' and 'second' force approaches of the time. The common ground of the humanistic approaches includes a focus on the potential of the human being for growth and psychological wellbeing. Preferring to use the term 'client' rather than 'patient' and coining the term 'counsellor', a 'third force' of psychology was brought into being. Thus, these three fundamental approaches and those who have refined and adapted them provide a basis for the 450-plus models of counselling and psychotherapy in existence today (McLeod, 2009), and the further reading at the end of the chapter gives suggestions of texts that can help you to learn about more of them. Of course, many counsellors and psychotherapists choose to work in an integrative or eclectic way, using two or more of these approaches to inform their therapeutic model. The profession continues to evolve. Transpersonal therapies, traditionally described under the humanistic umbrella, are more recently categorised as a 'fourth force'. Consideration of contemporary literature points to active attention given to pluralistic perspectives (Cooper and McLeod, 2011). This approach is based in humanistic and person-centred values, but encourages a range of responses to the client according to what has been demonstrated to work.

The chapter so far has demonstrated the organic growth of psychological therapies from pre-history to the present. Where traditionally counselling and psychotherapy might have been practised as an adjunct or addition to a medical role or another professional helping role, it is now viewed as a highly specialised field in its own right. The development of this as a distinct professional realm with diverse philosophical and theoretical underpinnings has direct links to the multitude of types and levels of training available today. Whether undergraduate or postgraduate, specialising in counselling or psychotherapy, the role of placement features centrally within the vast majority of recognised professional trainings.

Organisational settings – where is counselling and psychotherapy offered?

Over the past 50 years or so, there has become an increasing number and diversity of organisational settings in which the provision of therapy is being offered to both employees and/or service users. Many organisations provide placement opportunities to trainees or newly qualified practitioners. Consequently, it is possible to locate and secure placement experience within the public, private and voluntary sectors. Although services may be embedded within a related professional context, there are many organisations specialising in offering services which are solely counselling and psychotherapy based. Equally, opportunities within unrelated organisational settings provide a further source of placement potential. Generally speaking, counselling and psychotherapy literature offers scant attention to how the immediate organisational context may impact a practitioner's work, and even less consideration has been given to addressing the specific concerns of those seeking their initial or ongoing placement experience.

The **public sector**, also known as the 'state sector', refers to all aspects of our economy made up of organisations owned and controlled by the state or government. It consists of national and local governments, their agencies and chartered bodies, and deals directly with production, delivery and allocation of goods and services. Organisations within this sector have several key objectives to meet, including;

- ensuring the provision of an essential service
- providing a cost-effective service with wide-ranging availability
- maintaining services which are generally beneficial to society

The **private sector** incorporates those organisations owned and controlled by private individuals and groups, usually as a means of enterprise for profit. This sector incorporates several types of business; for example, sole trader, partnership, private limited company or public limited company. The central objectives within this sector tend to be:

- to survive in a competitive marketplace
- to maximise profits
- to make returns for their shareholders

The **voluntary sector** is a term used to describe organisations which focus on wider public benefit as opposed to statutory service delivery or profit. They are also known as 'third sector' or 'not for profit' organisations. The voluntary sector has several dimensions, ranging from small local groups to large international organisations, many of which have registered charity status. There are five distinguishing features which tend to be common to all voluntary sector organisations. These include that they are:

1. organised – having some decision-making structures
2. non-governmental – being institutionally separate from government
3. not for profit – in that generated profits are not distributed to members or directors
4. self-governing – free of the control from outside forces
5. voluntary – gaining some degree of benefit from voluntary contribution of time or money.

It is worth bearing in mind that organisations in all of the above sectors may solely provide counselling and psychotherapy, or conversely this may be one of a number of services offered. The experience of a trainee working in each will therefore vary, as the following vignette illustrates.

I work in a 'wellbeing' organisation which offers a range of health-related services to those who find themselves homeless. I am lucky that my line manager, although not a counsellor, has a good understanding of it and the differences between therapy and the other services offered by our agency. I have found that this is not always the case for some of my peers working in similar organisations. The added advantage of working here is that I get a great insight into multi-disciplinary working and have referral routes at my fingertips should more specialised services be required by my clients.

The nature of the placement organisation

If we imagine the placement as a living organism we gain insight into its nature and how it might be influenced by its internal and external environments. Just as a human being, animal or plant is influenced by internal biological and genetic factors, plus external influences such as quality of nutrition available, so the placement is influenced in similar ways. The environment impacting the placement is made up of both organisational (internal) and socio–political (external) factors (see Figure 1.1).

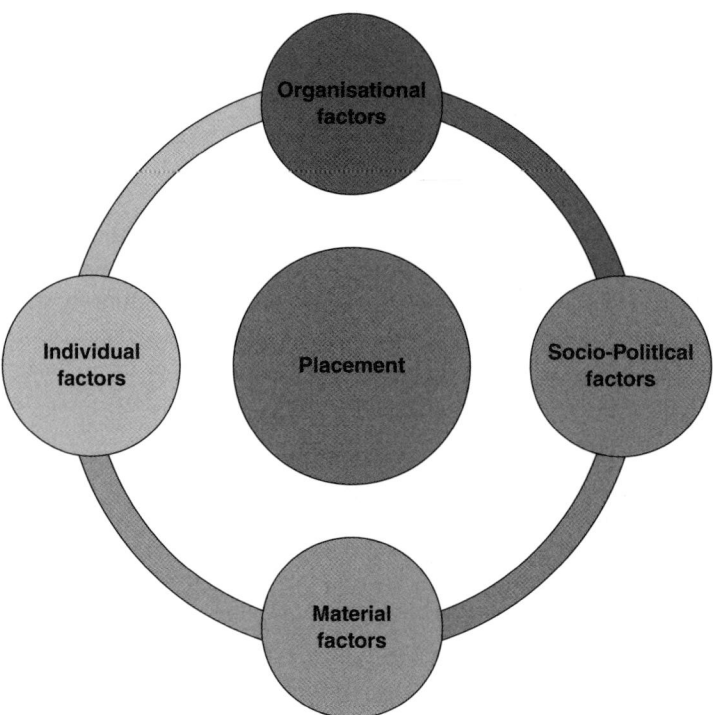

FIGURE 1.1   *Placement influences*

This section will examine these factors in turn, including what they constitute and how they influence provision in any particular context. The examples used will take the organisation as a starting point and consider how internal and external factors impact on whether a counselling service is provided at all, whether it offers placements to trainees, and if so how it might operate.

Internal influences

Internal influences upon a placement are multiple and so the suggested list below is not exhaustive.
   Internal influence may include:

- Material resources
  - premises
  - allocation of funding
- People resources
  - paid staff
  - voluntary staff
- Organisational resources
  - policies and procedures
  - staff systems and organisational structures

Material resources

Just as we depend upon our body to survive, so there are a number of material factors which will influence the survival and health of the placement.

Premises

The premises in which the organisation is located and the space available within it will influence whether a counselling/psychotherapy service can be offered. There may be no private rooms available, there may be several services competing for limited space, or the organisation may have to rent a small space within the premises of another organisation. If premises permit the offering of a counselling service, space may be one factor that dictates how many trainee placements can be offered, if this can be accommodated at all.

Allocation of funding

Funding will be discussed within 'External influences' below, since money to support an organisation has to come from somewhere! However, once secured and received by the organisation, funding will be allocated according to a multiplicity of factors. The amount of funding a counselling service receives, if any, will depend upon the stated purpose of the funding when applied for and approved. Additionally, the organisation may have priorities which remain consistent or change from year to year, perhaps according to local and national socio-political factors. This means that the 'pot' of money received by a counselling service within an organisation may fluctuate, influencing how many paid staff can be employed, how many volunteer counsellors can be supported, with a knock-on effect to how many clients can be seen. Thus, some counselling services operate time-limited services or waiting lists of various lengths depending upon the above factors. Equally, financial resources may determine whether free supervision can be offered to those undertaking a counselling/psychotherapy placement or if a placement fee is charged to cover this and any other administrative costs involved in managing a volunteer counsellor/therapist.

People resources – paid staff and volunteers

People are resources. The experience, knowledge and skills they bring to an organisation has the potential to both enhance and detract from its health. Organisations may employ solely paid staff, only use volunteers, or both. This balance will in part be dependent upon the material factors we have already mentioned. The difficulties organisations and counselling services face in finding suitably trained staff may impact upon their operation. For example, a counselling service serving a linguistic minority group may depend upon finding suitably trained employees or volunteers fluent enough in the specific language to be able to communicate with clients and service users directly without the use of interpreters. The use of interpreters would constitute an additional (potentially externally sourced) 'person' resource, and thus an additional expense.

All of the other socio-political factors we are considering have the potential to influence people's day-to-day experience within an organisation. For example, stress levels may be high when awaiting approval for an application for funding, and morale potentially low if funding bids fail, meaning services need to make cutbacks or, in more extreme circumstances cease operations.

Organisational resources

Policies and Procedures

In order to function well, organisations (as well as counselling services within them) benefit from clearly defined policies and procedures.

Clear knowledge of the policies and procedures of an organisation or service enables a therapist to be transparent with their client about the boundaries and contract from the outset of their relationship. This enables both the counsellor and the client to make informed choices based on the full information available.

Policies and procedures are not usually devised in isolation, but will be influenced by external factors such as legislation, ethical codes and frameworks of professional bodies and any organisational requirements. We have already discussed how factors such as financial resources and people resources may

> A **policy** can be defined as a principle or set of principles which guide the action of an individual or support their decision making within a particular organisational context. In contrast, a **procedure** is a defined set of actions or steps to be followed. Policies help us decide what to do; procedures tell us how it should be done.

influence policy in terms of the length of contract a service is able to offer to a client. Legislation will likely determine the parameters of an organisation's confidentiality policy, thereby impacting decisions made; for example, in regard to disclosing client material outside the therapy relationship. Policy, however, does not tell us how we would receive and deal with a client referral, or break confidentiality in the eventuality that this is necessary. For this information we would seek instruction from the procedures laid down by an organisation or service, support from other relevant colleagues within the organisation, our supervisor and ethical codes and frameworks of relevant professional bodies.

Staff systems and organisational structures

Within each organisation we have spoken about, staff, both paid and volunteer, will be organised according to a particular structure. Unless the organisation or service is completely egalitarian, the organisation of staff will usually be hierarchical. The structure within a counselling service will dictate who a trainee counsellor will report to (e.g. a counselling service manager). Within very small organisations staff may take on multiple roles, and this may lead to potential dual relationships which will need to be managed appropriately. For example, a volunteer's line manager may also take on the role of supervisor and be a counsellor themselves, meaning there are a number of relational roles to manage as a direct result of the particular structure of the service. Organisations within the charitable sector may have a board of trustees or a committee which maintains overall control and management of the organisation (Charity Commission UK, 2012).

> A **dual relationship** is created where one or more parties in a relationship have multiple roles in relation to one another; for example, client and friend, trainer and mentor, line manager and supervisor (Gabriel, 2005). According to BACP (2013), dual relationships can never be neutral and therefore require careful consideration by each party before entering into them (assuming prior knowledge) and review on an ongoing basis whilst duality of relationship continues.

External influences

External influences upon an organisation operate on three main levels; the social, the political and the cultural. It could be argued that there are many overlaps between these factors, and this is indeed the case. Equally, there are multiple overlaps and influences between the external factors, discussed in this section, and internal factors, discussed above. We will look at these influences, how they might impact the organisation, and thus the trainee's experience in placement.

Local socio-cultural factors

Each local geographic area has a particular demographic make-up; for example, it may be made up mainly of local authority and rented housing, or privately owned homes, or there may be a high number of refugees and asylum seekers settled within a particular postcode area. Factors such as these are likely to influence the type and nature of organisations and counselling services offering their services in the locality. It is likely, for example, that organisations wishing to offer psychotherapeutic services to asylum seekers and refugees will choose a location near to an area in which the client group is known to have settled: the socio-cultural environment has influenced the location of a particular counselling service.

Local and national government

Local and national government are also influential factors. Different political parties have different strategic priorities. The strategic priorities of the current local or national government will influence the types of projects which are supported financially through grants or funding. This means for example that it may be more likely to gain funding during the political term of one particular political party for services for children and young people. Following general or local election the political parties, and thus priorities, may change. It may then become more difficult for a service for young people to gain continuing funding, but conversely, easier for a service focussing upon rehabilitation of offenders to gain grant funding and thus be viable as an ongoing project.

International Factors

It is worth considering that the influence of external factors does not end at the shore or border of any particular country. For example, at the time of writing there is conflict occurring in Libya. Since Libya is one of the world's main oil producers this means that the price of oil, and thus motor fuel, is rising. Increases in fuel prices may have a detrimental impact upon the cost of a multitude of commodities due to increased cost of transportation. This means that the expenses of an organisation are increased, having the potential to cause financial struggles and impact upon internal structures.

Impact for the trainee

The impact for the trainee of such influences will be varied and multiple. There may, for example, be difficulty in gaining a placement with a particular client group. Trainees may find that applications for funding are undertaken, successfully or otherwise, during their time with an organisation, influencing the length of their placement contract. There may be the financial resources to provide supervision in-house, or trainees may need to pay for their own external supervision. In addition, it is likely that your previous experiences of working within organisational contexts will have an impact; for instance, in regard to your selection of placement or in regard to how you make sense of experiences once a placement has been secured. We invite you to consider your personal experiences in Activity 1.3 with the hope that this provides some material for further reflection when moving on to Chapter 2.

> ## Activity 1.3 Exploring organisational experience
>
> Aim
>
> - To reflect on personal experiences of working within organisational settings in order to consider the potential impact upon future placement experiences.
>
> Background
>
> There are implications for the therapeutic relationship and process – some helpful, others potentially detrimental – for counsellors and psychotherapists when working within organisational settings. These can take numerous forms and may include:
>
> - organisational dynamics
> - conflicts in roles
> - differences between the values of the organisation and those of therapy
> - competing expectations
> - stress and burnout.
>
> Activity
>
> With this in mind and using the following questions, we invite you to consider your own experiences in more detail, making note of your responses in whatever format you wish (e.g. journal writing or utilising creative media).
>
> - First, reflect on your experience of working within organisations. How do you describe these experiences? Is there anything that stands out as particularly rewarding? What challenges have you faced, and how did you respond to these?
> - How, if at all, do you think your experiences have influenced your decision to train as a therapist?
> - Are there any organisational settings that you would like to work within as a trainee therapist?
> - What challenges do you imagine facing in your preferred setting(s) and how might you manage these?
>
> *A PDF version of this activity is available to download from https://study.sagepub.com/oldaleandcooke*

Organisational settings

Apart from the categorisations of public, private and voluntary sectors we described earlier, the types of organisations you might find within each sector are too multifaceted to list in detail in this chapter. The further reading section gives some ideas about how you might investigate individual settings in more depth. To expand on what was mentioned previously, organisations under the public, private or voluntary umbrella fall under a number of categories, including, but not limited to:

- medical, including primary and secondary care, mental health and private healthcare settings
- educational, including primary, secondary, further, higher and private education
- workplace services, both within an organisation or an externally contracted employee assistance programme
- pastoral services, provided within a particular religious or spiritual context
- the Justice System, including prisons and probation services
- generalised counselling services, offering services for a range of issues and levels of complexity
- specialised counselling services, providing therapy for particular client groups such as survivors of sexual abuse, voice hearers and the bereaved. Factors such as gender, age and sexual orientation may also be a basis for provision to a specialist group.

Dependent on the context and availability of funds, services may be offered free to clients or they may be asked to pay for therapeutic services.

Chapter summary and ongoing reflections

This chapter has considered the historical origins of counselling and psychotherapy modalities as well as the development from pre-history of attitudes towards and treatment of mental distress. Types of counselling organisations have been considered along with the sectors in which they reside. It may now be useful to consider how what we have discussed throughout the chapter can influence the experience of being in placement from the point of view of both the client and the therapist. Activity 1.4 invites you to consolidate your understanding of the chapter by selecting real-life examples of organisations offering therapeutic services about which to consider the likely impact of historical, social and contextual influences.

Activity 1.4 Exploring placement contexts

Aim

- To consider potential placement organisations in light of the themes presented within Chapter 1.

Activity

Select one or two organisations offering counselling or psychotherapy services with which you are familiar. Next consider each of the column headings in Table 1.2, making note of your responses.

As you reflect on the chapter, revisit the ideas you captured in Activity 1.1. Has anything changed that you might now wish to add to your reflections?

TABLE 1.2 Exploring placement contexts grid

Chosen setting	Historical and social development of placement	Sector and likely funding sources	Likely referral sources	Types of client presenting issues	Reflections on impact of setting for client	Reflections on impact of setting for therapist
Setting 1						
Setting 2						

A PDF version of this activity is available to download from https://study.sagepub.com/oldaleandcooke

Chapter 2 invites you to consider your personal motivations to practise as well as supporting reflection in regard to your personal development, theoretical and ethical understanding. In this way it starts the process of assessing readiness to undertake the placement search. Before you move on, the below questions invite you to capture key aspects of your learning as well as any further points for action; you may wish to record your responses in your training journal or equivalent.

1. Record your thoughts and feelings as you come to the end of the chapter, with particular reference to the activities you have undertaken.
2. List one or two main areas of learning.
3. List points of action or further enquiry you will undertake in relation to any potential areas for further investigation, e.g. the chapter may have sparked an interest in learning about a different modality to the one in which you are training. Or you may be interested in learning more about a particular placement context or sector. The further reading section may be of help in this endeavour.
4. Set a deadline for yourself to undertake any actions you have highlighted in point 3 above.

Further reading

To learn more about the history of the Counselling and Psychotherapy professions and gain an overview of the three main counselling models – psychodynamic, cognitive behavioural therapy and humanistic – see *An Introduction to Counselling* by John McLeod (2009). Andrew Reeves' (2012) *An Introduction to Counselling and Psychotherapy* also gives an overview of these modalities as well as different counselling contexts. *Understanding Counselling and Psychotherapy* (Barker, Vossler and Langdridge, 2010) introduces further approaches such as existentialism, mindfulness, socio-cultural and systemic approaches to therapy. The SAGE Counselling in Action series (edited by Windy Dryden) can offer insight into many individual counselling models and professional and ethical issues. For anyone interested in integrative approaches to counselling, Lapworth and Sills' (2010) *Integration in Counselling and Psychotherapy* offers an overview. For more information on transpersonal approaches you might access John Rowan's (2005) text *The Transpersonal: Spirituality in Psychotherapy and Counselling*.

Further information can be gained about various counselling settings from Judy Moore and Ruth Roberts' (2010) text *Counselling and Psychotherapy in Organisational Settings*. The Counselling in Context series (Open University Press) edited by Moira Walker and Michael Jacobs covers pastoral, criminal justice, voluntary and workplace sectors. The Clinical Counselling in Context series (Routledge) edited by Peter Thomas, Suzan Davison and Christopher Rance also covers pastoral settings. This series also includes medical, primary care, further and higher education and voluntary and community settings.

References

Barker, M., Vossler, A. and Langdridge, D. (2010) *Understanding Counselling and Psychotherapy*. London: Sage/Open University Press.

Beveridge, A.W. and Renvoize, E.B. (1988) 'Electricity: a history of its uses in the treatment of mental illness in Britain during the second half of the 19th century', *British Journal of Psychiatry*, 153: 157–62.

Bond, T. (2010) *Standards and Ethics for Counselling in Action*, 3rd edn. London: Sage.

British Association for Counselling and Psychotherapy (BACP) (2013) *Ethical Framework for Good Practice in Counselling and Psychotherapy*. Available at: www.bacp.co.uk/admin/structure/files/pdf/9479_ethical%20framework%20jan2013.pdf (accessed 23.3.14).

Bynum, W. (2008) *The History of Medicine: A Very Short Introduction*. Oxford: Oxford University Press.

Charity Commision UK (2012) *The Essential Trustee: What You Need to Know*. Available at: www.charitycommission.gov.uk/detailed-guidance/trustees-staff-and-volunteers/the-essential-trustee-what-you-need-to-know-cc3/ (accessed 18.08.14).

Cooper, M. and McLeod, J. (2011) *Pluralistic Counselling and Psychotherapy*. London: Sage.

Doniger, W. and Eliage, M. (2004) *Shamanism: Archaic Techniques of Ecstasy*. Princeton, NJ: Princeton University Press.

Dryden, W. and Mytton, J. (1999) *Four Approaches to Counselling & Psychotherapy*. London: Routledge.

Gabriel, L. (2005) *Speaking the Unspeakable: The Ethics of Dual Relationships in Counselling and Psychotherapy*. Hove: Routledge.

Lapworth, P. and Sills, C. (2010) *Integration in Counselling and Psychotherapy: Developing a Personal Approach*. London: Sage.

McLeod, J. (2009) *An Introduction to Counselling*, 4th edn. Maidenhead: Open University Press.

Mearns, D. (1997) *Person-Centred Counselling Training*. London: Sage.

Moore, J. and Roberts, R.M. (2010) *Counselling and Psychotherapy in Organisational Settings*. Exeter: Learning Matters.

Porter, R. (2003) *Madness: A Brief History*. Oxford: Oxford University Press.

Reeves, A. (2012) *An Introduction to Counselling and Psychotherapy: From Theory to Practice*. London: Sage.

Rogers, C.R. (1942) *Counselling and Psychotherapy*. Cambridge, MA: Houghton Mifflin.

Rogers, A. and Pilgrim, D. (2010) *A Sociology of Mental Health and Illness*. Maidenhead: Oxford University Press.

Rowan, J. (2005) *The Transpersonal: Spirituality in Psychotherapy and Counselling*. London: Routledge.

Shorter, E. (1997) *A History of Psychiatry: From the Era of the Asylum to the Age of Prozac*. New York: Wiley.

Two

Preparing for Placement: Personal, Theoretical and Ethical Considerations

This chapter will:

- Support you to consider your competence as a trainee therapist thus far, whilst facilitating reflection in relation to your fitness to practise through structured reflection on personal and professional perspectives including:
  - motivations to become a counsellor/psychotherapist
  - understanding of the philosophical and theoretical underpinnings of your chosen psychotherapeutic model
  - ethical knowledge and understanding
  - personal development and its intrinsic links to your professional development
  - unique circumstances (e.g. family and work commitments) and how these may both impact and be impacted by the practicalities of starting placement and undertaking supervision of therapeutic work.

The distinction between competence and fitness was outlined in the Introduction. Briefly, **competence** refers to the knowledge and ability to be able to undertake a particular endeavour. **Fitness** is a wider notion which includes considerations, such as, personal wellbeing and circumstances which should be evaluated alongside competence in the overall process of decision making about readiness to commence in placement.

The process of identifying and arranging a suitable counselling or psychotherapy placement is primarily the responsibility of the trainee therapist. However, the specific requirements in regard to searching for and securing your placement will likely vary according to the availability of placements in your area, the structure of your training programme and the ways in which placement providers are approved by your training organisation. In Chapter 1, we considered the placement organisation, including various factors which dictate its nature. You were invited to consider the implications of working in specific placement contexts. Here, we build on this discussion by placing you centrally within the placement endeavour. We facilitate exploration of your understanding of various components of what it means to be a therapist and the potential implications of these factors in regard to your readiness to begin the placement search and their impact on your work as a trainee therapist. Reflection is invited through structured activities related to your personal circumstances, development and motivations to join this profession. In addition, focus is given to the consideration of ethics as well as your growing understanding of theoretical perspectives and the principles underpinning these. Thus, opportunities to identify your personal strengths and areas for development are provided.

The subsequent chapter considers training provider and wider professional requirements in order to support reflection upon further significant factors. It is our hope that the groundwork undertaken within each of these chapters will support you in consideration of your own readiness to commence client work outside of the training context and stand you in good stead for the placement search and application process which is considered in Chapter 4. Our rationale for inviting such extensive pre-placement reflection is primarily underpinned by the fundamental importance of ethical and reflexive practice.

Your personal values and viewpoints are likely to contribute to choices made in regard to practice; this can be traced back to the starting point of your training journey as it is highly probable that these were central to the process of selecting an approach in which to train. For instance, those who emphasise the subjective nature of human experience and the importance of personal freedom may have chosen to study approaches such as gestalt, person-centred or experiential-process,

> Reflexivity might be defined as 'action on reflection'. Tosey and Gregory (2002: 138) suggest that it is the fusion of being aware of our 'motivations, assumptions, thoughts and feelings' along with applying and acting on these in the world.

whereas others may have selected a psychoanalytic training due to its emphasis on the relevance of the unconscious. Further to this, personal perspectives and those valued within the modality in which you are training will inevitably translate into theoretical ideas. The basis of this, in turn, may inform a particular ethical stance and thus impact your ethical considerations and decision making. Having said this, some ethical decisions may be less influenced by the approach of the practitioner; for example, a factor that runs through the ethical codes and/or frameworks of the major professional bodies within the therapy world is the necessity for each practitioner to recognise the limits of their competence (e.g. BACP, 2013; UKCP, 2009). Equally there are laws such as the Prevention of Terrorism Act (2005), the Children Act (2004) (with specific reference to safeguarding children) and the Equality Act (2010), which will have a direct impact upon organisational context and ultimately the decisions made by the practitioner in particular circumstances. However, because contemporary ethical codes and frameworks tend to be principle- rather than rule-based, some ethical decisions are open to interpretation. For instance, the idea of what constitutes 'autonomy' (BACP, 2013) may be influenced by the stance taken in regard to ideas about the therapist's role in facilitating change. This in turn arises from the approach in which you are training. Where in some models the introduction of therapist interpretation or technique into the client relationship may be embraced; it may be critiqued by practitioners from other modalities as detracting from client autonomy and self-determination. We strongly believe that practitioners are individuals and will arrive at their own position in relation to how their value systems and theoretical understanding influences their ethical stance; we see this process as a key aspect of practitioner development in which placement-based experience plays a central role.

We suggest that self-reflection in regard to the areas we have identified supports the foundation of ethical practice, providing a solid basis in preparation for placement and ultimately throughout your professional career. In terms of the placement search, it will ensure that you are searching for a placement in which you can practise comfortably from your own position, or pre-empt any challenges to your philosophical, theoretical and ethical stance. In considering your personal and professional development, we seek to enable you to think about your own robustness as a practitioner as you embark on the placement search. A consideration of the practicalities of your life allows you to set a firm foundation for the additional demands which will inevitably be placed upon your time and resources. At the end of the chapter we provide further opportunity to review your learning in order to support you to identify ways in which you can apply any insight gained in relation to your assessment of readiness and commencement of placement.

Personal and professional motivations

Consideration of personal motivation to become a therapist tends to be paramount to the selection process on counselling and psychotherapy training programmes. For you, as a trainee therapist, there are key reasons why this is important. Counselling and psychotherapy are relational processes, and every aspect of our being, including our motivation for what we do, influences our work with clients. This influence has the potential to help and/or hinder the process of therapy, and to provide an environment conducive to positive therapeutic outcome, or one with the potential to harm both the therapist and the client.

Authors including Sussman (2007) and Bager-Charleson (2010) suggest that a multitude of reasons can underlie our decision to become a therapist. These are unique to the individual and are likely to comprise of a combination of factors including, but not limited to:

- a genuine interest in people
- the need/desire for a career change
- impact of a significant life event
- a desire to understand self and others
- altruistic reasons
- resolution of personal, developmental or relational processes
- reasons of personal satisfaction (feel-good factor)
- self-punishment linked to emotional demands of therapeutic work
- fulfilment of a need to relate not met (or met at insufficient depth) in personal life.

What is common in both Bager-Charleson (2010) and Sussman's (2007) writing is an acknowledgement that the decision to become a therapist is just one way in which factors such as those above gain expression. A neutral stance is taken in that the practitioner is encouraged to identify and explore their motivations without attributing positive or negative value judgements to any of them. We suggest that this facilitates a dynamic reflexivity, self-awareness in action, which is vital for you to consider before undertaking placement and which will continue throughout your therapeutic career. With all of the above in mind, Activity 2.1 invites you to explore your personal motivations for training as a therapist.

Activity 2.1 Consideration of motivations to practise

Aims

- To facilitate identification of and reflection in regard to your motivations to practise as a therapist.
- To consider the potential impact of your motivations on the placement search process and future work with clients.

Background

Consideration of personal motivation to become a therapist tends to be paramount to the selection process on counselling and psychotherapy training programmes. As a trainee therapist, there are key reasons why this is important; for instance, counselling and psychotherapy are relational processes and every aspect of our being, including our motivations for what we do, have the potential to impact client work. This influence has the potential to help and/or hinder the process of therapy: to provide an environment conducive to positive therapeutic outcome, or one with the potential to harm both the therapist and the client. Identification of and reflection upon your motivations is likely to support your professional development in numerous ways, including aiding preparation for securing and undertaking a placement.

Activity

- Take some time to think about and note down your reasons and motivations for training as a therapist. Do not edit your responses at this stage. In this way you are likely to uncover a whole host of driving factors.
- Keep asking yourself 'why this reason?' until you feel all ideas have been exhausted – you may have uncovered factors apparent at the outset or you may have discovered something new.
- Note your personal responses to each motivating factor.
- Once you have reached what you feel to be the root(s) of your motivation, take some time to consider and note down how these factors may:
    - impact upon the placement search process
    - help and/or hinder your relationships with future clients
    - support and/or pose risk to your own wellbeing.

A PDF version of this activity is available to download from https://study.sagepub.com/oldaleandcooke

Motivation to work with a particular group or area of concern

Generalised therapeutic services are available across the spectrum of organisations presented in Chapter 1 and might include work in GP surgeries or in a local counselling centre. Specialised services include the provision of counselling/psychotherapy to a particular societal group (e.g. gender, ethnicity) or to those who have had particular experiences in their life (e.g. bereavement or trauma). Although you may be certain of the areas in which you wish to work, there are likely to be benefits gained from careful consideration in regard to the selection of client group and/or presenting issues. For example, explorations undertaken with your supervisor (if you have one), trainers or peers could support you in uncovering any underlying or unconscious motivations, ensuring that these are taken into account when considering possible effects on self and future client work. In some instances, such exploration may lead you to make an evaluation of your fitness such that you decide to delay working within a particular area until personal work can be undertaken to resolve issues which might impede your ability to forge a therapeutic alliance or effective relationship. Equally, considerations might strengthen your resolve to seek a placement with a particular client group as you can clearly identify that you have much to offer to clients and/or work colleagues in terms of passion, motivation and knowledge. As the following example shows, motivations to work as a therapist and with a particular group are rarely neutral in their nature and can have an impact upon the client and/or therapist involved.

Shortly into my first placement I realised that working with the linguistic minority and cultural group I had grown up within was not as clear-cut a decision as I had first thought. I had always wanted to give something back to this community, and since I am bilingual, practising in this area had seemed like it was the perfect niche for me, a logical first step in my journey as a therapist. However, I'd not realised the full impact of having grown up between two cultures. Since personal therapy for me was a relatively new thing I had only just started to work through the effect of this on all areas of my life and processes.

Whilst working with clients I started to notice that I was making erroneous interpretations of their material based on my own assumptions. This was undoubtedly influenced by some of my childhood experiences. I also noticed that I had a tendency to rescue the client because of my own perception of the discriminated position of my native cultural group in society. Luckily, with the help of a great therapist and supervisor I was able to work these issues through on a professional and personal level. The tendencies are still there, I think they always will be, but they are in my awareness now and I can spot their influence in my client relationships more quickly and act before they become a problem.

Had the above trainee therapist completed Activity 2.1 they undoubtedly would have listed 'giving back to their cultural group' as one of their motivations to work as a therapist. Further exploration may have identified key factors within their personal experience related to issues of power and the identification of this cultural group as being discriminated against within society. Could taking on the role of therapist have been motivated, in part, by the desire to redress the power balance through perceived empowerment of this particular client group? Might this be seen as resolution of a relational process as we suggested earlier when discussing Sussman (2007) and Bager-Charleson's (2010) work? If taken to supervision, the long-term impact of the trainee therapist's tendency to rescue might have been explored, including reflection related to how this might have, in extreme circumstances, led to potential boundary mismanagement such as overstepping the role of the therapist and taking on other support roles such as interpreter. The trainee might have considered how this rescuing could be detrimental to upholding the BACP principles of autonomy, beneficence and non-maleficence (BACP, 2013).

We can therefore see how careful pre-placement reflection in relation to motivations may have supported this trainee therapist to make an informed decision about if and how to proceed with their plans to work with this particular client group. Having said this, you may already be in placement, in which case much can be gained from continuing reflection with those in your support network as to the impact of your motivations on your own wellbeing and client work. Indeed, ongoing and retrospective reflection is inevitable and is something we will continue to encourage throughout this book.

Whilst some trainee therapists, as we have illustrated, will have a clear idea of the client group they want to work with, many decide to keep their options open with the view to securing a broad range of experience in their first placement. This can allow the idea of specialist work to be revisited later, with the benefit of experience gained from the accumulation of client hours. Additionally, revision of professional direction might be considered in the light of experience gained. It is worth noting that specialist services and, therefore, placements within these contexts tend to be limited and breaking into a specialist field can be difficult although not impossible. Those trainees wishing to work with specific client groups are sometimes fortunate in securing a placement in their area of interest. They may already work in or have contacts in the field which aids the process as the following example demonstrates.

In my first career I work as a 'carer' of young people with learning difficulties. I knew that the organisation I worked for had a counselling service based across the city and I wondered if they might be willing to take an application from me. After considering with my manager and supervisor the implications of having two roles within the same organisation, and how dual roles with clients might be prevented, I decided this was manageable and applied to the service. I felt I had a head start in this placement as I knew the particular difficulties faced by the client group and was familiar with the organisation, their aims and internal politics. I later took on another placement to broaden my experience, but am grateful to my work organisation for supporting me in this first step as a counsellor.

So your exploration and decision making at this stage is about why you want to undertake work as a therapist, including motivations to practise with particular groups of people or issues of concern. Reflecting on this prior to securing a placement can assist you to identify any motivations which might be problematic; for example, personally, in regard to the therapeutic relationship and/or organisational context (you may wish to revisit your reflections in regard to Activity 1.3 which focused upon your organisation experience), thereby enabling you to embark on further exploration before you commence the search for a placement. Equally, active exploration can facilitate identification of strengths and support you to utilise these to your advantage when applying to placement providers (see Chapter 4). You might, following the exploration in this section, have a clearer idea about whether it is most appropriate to search for a placement offering services to a particular client group or to broaden your search.

Personal and professional readiness

The previous section supported you to explore your motivations to train as a psychotherapist or counsellor. This section looks at the assessment of your readiness to undertake this endeavour from a variety of perspectives. The question 'Am I ready?' encompasses notions of both competence and fitness, and starts and ends with you as an individual trainee. Whilst readiness to practise may be assessed in various ways by training organisations, supervisors and placement organisations, it is only you who can truly know if you are ready to start client work based on honest and thorough personal reflection. Even if you have been assessed as ready, for instance, by your training organisation, a nagging doubt may remain which we would encourage you

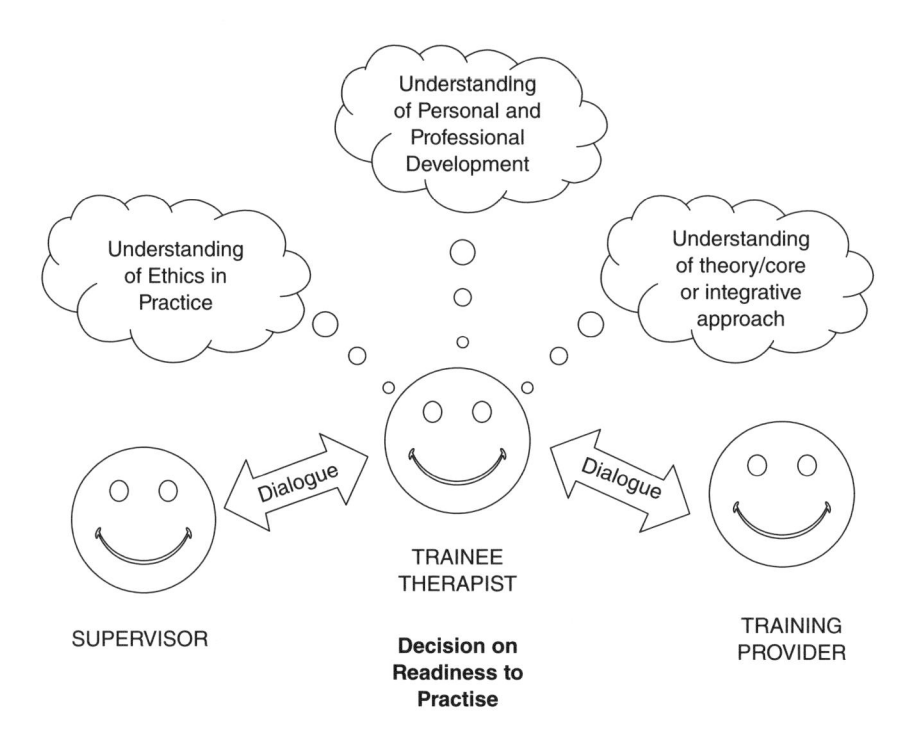

FIGURE 2.1 *The decision-making process*

to take seriously and explore. Equally you may be absolutely sure you are ready to commence client work, and later activities will give you an opportunity to rationalise this.

There are a number of other professionals who can support you with this decision-making process. For instance, your training provider may have a formal readiness to practise assessment process, ensuring ethical reflection in regard to both competence and fitness. This process may incorporate peer and tutor feedback to help decide whether you are sufficiently prepared to begin working with 'actual' clients in placement. It may also include reflection on some of the personal, theoretical and ethical points we suggest later in this chapter as well as a more formal observation of your therapeutic work. Your supervisor (if you have one at this stage) can support your reflective process and give guidance as to the appropriateness or otherwise of imminently searching and applying for a placement. These factors are considered further in Chapter 4. The following sections constitute a number of areas for consideration which can be undertaken in collaboration with your supervisor and training provider. Figure 2.1 illustrates what this collaborative discussion might look like.

Starting with the person of the trainee, and utilising activities along the way, the next sections consider a number of personal, professional and practical aspects of the readiness to practise decision-making process.

Reflecting on philosophical and theoretical understanding

All approaches to counselling and psychotherapy have explicit or implicit ideas which attempt to explain human nature and interaction. As such, it is inevitable that your training will incorporate consideration of the philosophical underpinnings of your chosen therapeutic modality together with how these manifest in the ideas that emerge in the theories you are learning about. This is illustrated metaphorically by the UK Association of Humanistic Psychology Practitioners (UKAHPP) (cited in Whitton, 2003: xii), who suggest that theory can be likened to a map of the ground of what it means to be human. There are many theoretical maps both within and outside of the humanistic tradition. However, no map *is* the

> Put simply, philosophy is:
>
> - the study of the fundamental nature of knowledge, reality and existence.
> - a theory or attitude that acts as a guiding principle for behaviour.
>
> And a theory can be seen as:
>
> - a supposition or a system of ideas intended to explain something.
> - a set of principles on which the practice of an activity is based.
>
> (Oxford Dictionary Online)

actual territory and experience of being human. Just as a map of London will never be London itself, so the map we use to navigate the client–therapist relationship is not the *actual* relationship in which we engage.

> McLeod (2009: 59–60) suggests a number of alternative metaphors for 'theory', which you may also find useful:
>
> - *building* an understanding or explanation
> - an explanatory *structure* or *framework*
> - *illuminating/shining* a light on something that is unclear
> - a *lens* that focuses on certain pieces of information
> - a *mirror* of nature
> - a *tool* for action
> - getting a *handle* on a confusing issue
> - a *network* of ideas
> - a *conversation* or *dialogue* between different perspectives.

In counselling and psychotherapy these maps can logically be broken down into two parts: a set of principles and theories in regard to what it means to be a person (a theory of Self); and another which attempts to illustrate therapy in action. The 'theory of Self' constitutes ideas about:

- what it means to be a person
- how human beings develop
- how emotional/psychological/behavioural distress occurs
- how this distress might be alleviated.

The 'theory of therapy' suggests how the way of working, as undertaken by the therapist, can support the process of change in the client and is closely linked to ideas suggested in the theory of Self inherent within the therapy model.

The modality in which you are training will have particular ideas about the above, or will integrate ideas from a number of approaches. Consequently, your understanding of underlying principles and key theoretical perspectives will in part be influenced by whether your training is based on one core philosophical and theoretical model (e.g. psychodynamic, cognitive behavioural, person-centred) or takes either an integrative or eclectic approach to therapy.

> The integrative therapist is one who practises from a number of potentially theoretically diverse disciplines. Integrationism is different from eclecticism in that the integrative therapist will 'emphasise the need for conceptual unity' (Feltham and Dryden, 1993: 94), whereas the eclectic therapist will draw from two or more models dependent upon client need (ibid: 56).

It is our experience and view that no matter which model you ascribe to, it is inevitable that ideas and the values or attitudes which they convey will have a direct impact upon your work as a practitioner.

> I chose a training based on humanistic perspectives as these seemed to represent some of the things I think are important to people overall. However, my trainer says that I should 'hold these theories lightly' when I'm working with clients. Why, then, is it important for me to think about my understanding of underpinning principles and theories before I start in placement? How will this reflection help me in determining whether I am ready to work with clients? And how might it support my placement search?

It seems reasonable to ask why we would include an evaluation of philosophical and theoretical understanding as part of your process of assessing your competence and readiness to start looking for a placement. In consideration of this, we return to the earlier metaphor of theory as a map of the ground. When embarking on the therapeutic relationship it would seem wise to use a map which is fit for purpose, one that sits well with us as a person and the client with whom we are working within the placement context. So we would suggest that developing a 'map' that works well for you (which can be 'held lightly') and having a *good enough* understanding of the ground it represents means that you are in a better position to start the journey with each unique client and in a potentially diverse placement context. Far from viewing this as a 'one time only' process, we suggest that you revisit your understanding of theory throughout your career as a therapist in a cyclical process of reflection.

> One way to undertake this reflection might be to assess theory and the need for further learning via the cycle suggested by Kolb (1984), which we highlighted in the Introduction.
>
> - Concrete experience – the reading of the chapter and engagement with activities.
> - Reflective observation – capturing key learning points and reflection in regard to activities.
> - Abstract conceptualisation – concluding your learning from the experience and making points for action.
> - Active experimentation – setting goals, objectives and timeframes for any further action or learning you wish to undertake.

I've read about research which indicates that the modality practised by the therapist is low on the scale of factors which contribute to positive therapeutic change. Is my understanding of theory really going to make me a better therapist and mean I'm more ready to start seeing clients?

We suggest taking a wider view of the potential use of these research findings because the relevance of your pre-placement reflection is multi-faceted, with approach-specific factors being only one component of influence on the provision of counselling and psychotherapy within your future placement(s).

Asay and Lambert (1999) do indeed cite that only 15 per cent of positive outcome in therapy is attributable to therapist technique or model factors. They also offer further insight into the factors that contribute to positive outcome, citing client variables and the relationship between the therapist and client as being significant (40 per cent and 30 per cent respectively). A further 15 per cent is attributed to placebo, hope and expectancy. Figure 2.2 illustrates these four factors.

Central to all four factors are the persons and the purpose involved in the endeavour. For example, meaning making and determining course of action are likely to be important; these are strongly influenced by what is valued by both parties and the ideas used to construct narrative and plans. Thus, meaning making and course of action may be influenced by one, all or a combination of the following:

- the values and ideals of the therapist (including, for instance, the theory of Self and therapy they adopt)

[Pie chart]

- Client/Extratherapeutic 40%
- Relationship 30%
- Model or Technique 15%
- Placebo, hope and expectancy 15%

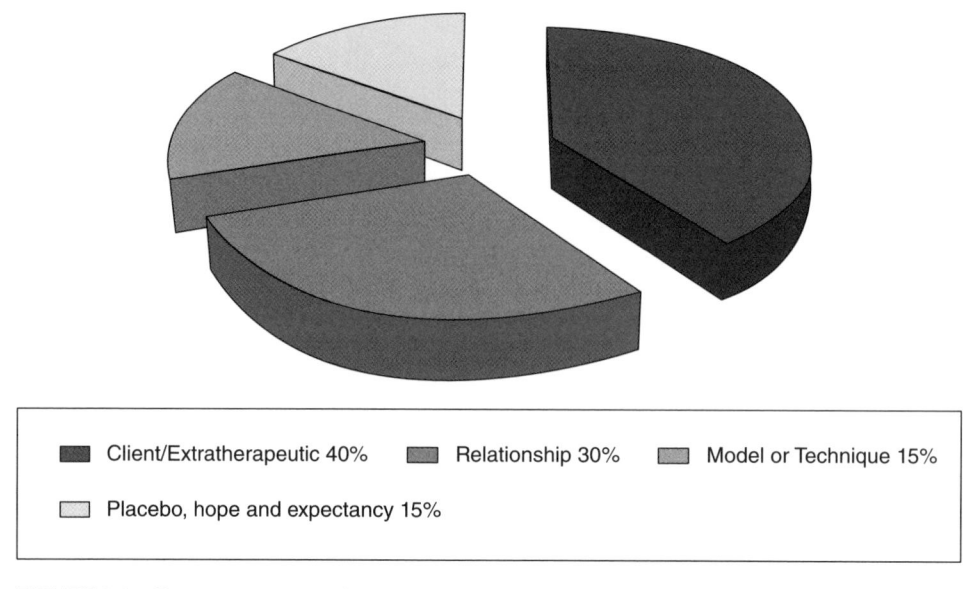

FIGURE 2.2 *Factors accounting for change in therapy (Asay & Lambert, 1999)*

- multiple client factors (including but not limited to their beliefs, values, needs, hopes for therapy, experiences of Self, others and the world)
- organisational factors (e.g. mission and aims)
- interactions with others in the field (peers, trainers, supervisors, etc.) who may hold similar, complementary or somewhat contradictory ideas.

Consequently, we are advocating that consideration be given to this area and the possible ways in which these elements of your developing knowledge and understanding might have relevance to your readiness to practise, the factors you are likely to encounter in selecting and working within a placement organisation, and ultimately the choices you will make when working with clients. With this in mind, Activity 2.2 provides some areas for personal consideration.

Activity 2.2 Considering philosophical and theoretical understanding

Aims

- To enable reflection in regard to your understanding of key theoretical components that underpin practice within the modality in which you are training.
- To facilitate consideration of the ways in which theoretical understanding supports your assessment of your readiness to undertake placement.

> ### Background
>
> All approaches to psychotherapy have explicit or implicit theories that attempt to explain human nature and interaction. These theories can be broken down into two parts: a set of principles in regard to what it means to be a person (a theory of Self); and another which attempts to illustrate therapy in action. These will be influenced by your own values and ideals.
>
> ### Activity
>
> How is the model of Self and therapy to which you ascribe influenced by the following:
>
> - concrete life experiences
> - philosophical ideas
> - religious and spiritual beliefs
> - political ideologies
> - ways of expressing yourself creatively
> - anything else which feels personally relevant and important.
>
> Consider the impact of the above in relation to these questions:
>
> - How might this be supportive of your readiness to commence placement and begin working with clients?
> - How might this impede your readiness to begin work with clients in placement?
>
> *A PDF version of this activity is available to download from https://study.sagepub.com/oldaleandcooke*

What then, have you learned about your own practice as it sits with your personal values, and those of the approach you are training in? How do these ideas influence you in training and practice, and how might they influence your decision making in the search for placement? Would you feel most comfortable searching for a placement whose philosophical base sits closely with your own? Or might you welcome the challenge of working with a more philosophically diverse group of practitioners? What might the advantages and disadvantages be of each? We hope that these reflections provide food for thought about the philosophical and theoretical basis of the placement you decide to search for. The following example illustrates some of the above points in conclusion of this section.

In thinking about where I wanted to work within placement and what I needed to learn about my chosen approach, I decided to apply to a provider which offered approach-specific opportunities to counselling trainees. I also widened my search to incorporate organisations whose mission statement reflected some of the underlying principles I hold as important, such as relating to the whole person rather than putting people into boxes or treating just symptoms related to a specific diagnosis.

My first placement was with an agency providing opportunities to both qualified and trainee therapists from a number of diverse modalities. I found this really challenging for a while. I found the offering, in my supervision group, of alternative perspectives to what might be going on for me or my client quite hard at first, feeling it was a challenge to my principles, theoretical understanding and style of working as a therapist. I had to work hard to translate what was being said into a format I understood and could relate to. However, as time went on there was a growing sense of mutuality and respect within our working relationships, which made the process progressively easier. I found myself more open to considering ideas which did not readily fit with my own, and I think my colleagues also became increasingly eager to hear ideas from my perspective. With hindsight, this collaborative process allowed me to learn more (unwittingly, perhaps) about other theories and perspectives, which will be invaluable when working with other professionals in future. It has also allowed me to evaluate the relevance of the other theories to my own way of working, and has, I hope, enriched my practice through the incorporation of some of these ideas as well as the rejection of those I could not reconcile with my own values.

Reflecting on ethical awareness

Ethics underpins every decision made by the therapist; for this reason, it is important that each practitioner comes to their own understanding of ethics as a concept, how it impacts personally and professionally, and how this is likely to influence the therapeutic relationship. Before going further, it might be useful to spend some time thinking about ethics as an idea and the associations it holds for you. Activity 2.3 poses some questions that facilitate this reflection and provide a basis for the continuing discussion in this section.

Activity 2.3 Reflections on 'ethics' in preparation for placement

Aim

- To facilitate reflection in regard to your associations with the word 'ethics' and how this might be linked to ethics in practice.
- To consider how these reflections might inform your assessment of readiness to begin working with clients.

Background

Ethical considerations, arguably, underpin every decision made by therapists. Personal values and moral viewpoints are likely to shape your approach as a therapist in a variety of ways. For this reason, it is important that each practitioner develops their own understanding in regard to ethics, including how this might impact the therapeutic relationship.

Preparing for Placement: Personal, Theoretical and Ethical Considerations

Activity

- Reflect upon the word **ethics**. What images or memories come to mind?
- Make a note of thoughts and feelings evoked for you as you reflect on this word and your initial responses.
- Do any associated words come to mind, and how are they similar and/or different?
- How are your responses/ideas linked to your own values and morals?
- How might your responses to the above impact your therapeutic work?
- What are the implications of these reflections in regard to your readiness to begin searching for and working in placement?

A PDF version of this activity is available to download from https://study.sagepub.com/oldaleandcooke

Whilst ethics itself is a philosophical idea about what constitutes right or wrong, it can be applied in many areas including psychotherapy and counselling. Evaluating your own ethical understanding is an essential pre-placement consideration. The practitioner who is working ethically is likely to have a heightened awareness of:

- their own values and beliefs
- the values of the profession as laid out in ethical codes and frameworks (such as UKCP and BACP)
- an awareness of the law as it may relate to counselling and psychotherapy practice (both generally and in relation to any particular client group the therapist may wish to work with)
- how the above factors interact, complement and potentially conflict with each other.

An understanding of ethics goes wider still and includes consideration of cultural and institutional norms, together with organisation-specific policies and procedures as well as the law of the country in which we work. In addition, it may be influenced by the philosophical and theoretical assumptions inherent in the model of therapy in which you are training.

Of course, it is impossible for a therapist to have advance knowledge of the ethical implications of every scenario or ethical dilemma

Ethics is a complex philosophical field with a number of branches, approaches and applications both in the psychotherapeutic field and beyond. Two approaches of particular interest to therapists, and which might influence ethical decision making (in addition) to the factors we have mentioned are **deontological** and **utilitarian** approaches. Bond describes these approaches thus: 'The deontological approach is based on deducing ethical obligations from a particular set of beliefs about the nature of reality. These obligations are viewed as universal and can be typified by treating people as ends in themselves. In contrast, the utilitarian approach is founded on an evaluation of the consequences of any action and can be typified by a commitment to achieving "the greatest good for the greatest number". The choice between the two systems can be represented as a choice between viewing people as ends in themselves or as the means to an end' (2010: 49). Although an in-depth discussion of these models is beyond the scope of this text, we suggest these may be useful ideas to keep in mind as you work through the chapter and as you begin working in placement.

they might come across before starting in placement. However, developing the capacity to consider the many factors at play avoids the eventuality of knee-jerk reactions when faced with complex ethical situations in client work. Therefore we are suggesting that you consider ethical thinking as a *process* rather than a static set of codes and frameworks, policies and procedures. Readiness to practise might, in part then, be evaluated by your willingness and confidence to engage in this process, given all of its complexity. You, as the trainee therapist, and your client reside at the heart of this process, at the centre of a system which involves all of the factors we have mentioned. Your job is to negotiate this process in a way which best takes account of all the factors involved.

Indeed, one of the first ethical decisions you need to make is that of whether you are ready to practise. Activity 2.4 provides you with an opportunity to consider the ethical dimension in regard to your decision as to whether this is the right time to start in placement.

Activity 2.4 Ethical considerations in the readiness to practise assessment process

Aim

- To promote ethical consideration of the perspectives of the various stakeholders involved as part of an overall assessment of readiness to commence placement.

Background

Readiness to practise might, in part, be evaluated by your willingness and confidence to engage in a process of ethical decision making, given all of its complexity, the systems and factors involved. One of the first ethical decisions you need to make is that of whether you are ready to practise.

Activity

- Put yourself in the role of the different stakeholders in the placement process:

    o yourself
    o your training provider
    o the placement provider
    o the client
    o the supervisor
    o professional bodies such as UKCP and BACP.

- What do you think each stakeholder is looking for in regard to your ethical awareness and capacity to engage with the process of ethical decision making in order to be confident that you are ready to start work with clients?
- Given what you have identified, how might you demonstrate your readiness to each stakeholder?

- Use these reflections to write a short paragraph outlining key elements of your ethical awareness and willingness to engage in the process of ethical decision making.
- Are there any areas which need further development and consideration? How might you facilitate this?

A PDF version of this activity is available to download from https://study.sagepub.com/oldaleandcooke

We hope that the ideas generated by this activity provide scope for further collaborative discussion with your peers, trainers and supervisors about your readiness to practise. The statement of ethical awareness you construct as part of the process of the above activity may be usefully reconsidered when we think about the application and interview process in Chapter 4. For example, some interview questions may be based upon your capacity to engage in ethical decision-making processes, including addressing ethical dilemmas. Equally, the decision about which placements you are willing to apply to may, in part, be influenced by significant aspects of their policy on ethical decision making. This also links back to our previous discussion about values. Now may be a useful time to revisit the ethical codes or frameworks outlined by any professional bodies of which you are a member as well as those advocated by your training provider and/or potential placement providers. We hope the ideas presented within this sub-section enable you to reflect on these codes or frameworks afresh with a view to how these might support you in the placement search, application process and your early and ongoing practice.

Reflecting on personal development

Whilst personal development cannot be wholly separated from the theoretical and ethical considerations we have discussed so far, it is worthy of some attention in its own right. There are numerous reasons why personal development is important for you as a therapist. In our earlier discussion in relation to personal motivations, we indicated that all aspects of the therapist have the potential to impact upon the therapeutic relationship and process. Thorne and Dryden go as far as to suggest that 'an unaware counsellor leading an unexamined life is likely to be a liability rather than an asset' (1991: 4). Various authors in the field highlight the importance of the development of the therapist. McLeod cites 'personal soundness' as a key competency of the counsellor, which includes '[a]bsence of personal needs or irrational beliefs that are destructive to counselling relationships, self-confidence, capacity to tolerate strong or uncomfortable feelings in relation to clients, secure personal boundaries, ability to be a client. Absence of social prejudice, ethnocentrism and authoritarianism' (2009: 613). Indeed, if the relationship is as critical to therapeutic outcome as Asay and Lambert (1999) suggest (see earlier section on theoretical understanding, p. 33), the development of the therapist as an integral part of that relationship is central and personal soundness, as suggested by McLeod (2009), could be considered vital.

Most training programmes will encourage you to assess your development periodically, perhaps engaging peers and tutors as part of this process. Personal therapy and supervision, as well as a number of other aspects of training, will likely support your continuing personal and professional development. However, as with assessment of theoretical understanding and ethical awareness, we stress the importance of individual responsibility when considering competence and fitness to practise lies first and foremost with the individual. Activity 2.5 is just one way in which you might undertake your own assessment of your development and 'personal soundness' as part of your overall assessment of readiness to start work with clients.

Activity 2.5 Considering personal development and readiness to practise

Aim

- To enable reflection on personal development and 'soundness' as part of an overall assessment of readiness to practise.

Background

Thorne and Dryden suggest that 'an unaware counsellor leading an unexamined life is likely to be a liability rather than an asset' (1991: 4). McLeod cites 'personal soundness' as a key competency of the counsellor which includes '[a]bsence of personal needs or irrational beliefs that are destructive to counselling relationships, self-confidence, capacity to tolerate strong or uncomfortable feelings in relation to clients, secure personal boundaries, ability to be a client. Absence of social prejudice, ethnocentrism and authoritarianism' (2009: 613).

Activity

- Consider yourself at the beginning of training or at the beginning of this academic year. What were your main strengths and areas for personal development? You might use McLeod's definition of 'personal soundness' above to guide your thinking.
- Use specific examples from the training context and/or personal therapy to show how you have:
  - used your strengths constructively in a relationship
  - worked actively on your areas for development.

These examples might include specific feedback you have received from your peers and trainers.

- Turning your attention to your current developmental agenda, what areas for development remain? How might these elements impact upon your readiness to start work with clients?
- Identify constructive ways in which you might work with your ongoing areas for development.

A PDF version of this activity is available to download from https://study.sagepub.com/oldaleandcooke

As with Activity 2.4, the material you generate in undertaking this activity will be useful to revisit in Chapter 4 when we consider aspects of the placement application process. For instance, many application forms will ask you to outline your strengths and areas for development. Highlighting these now enables you to enter into collaborative discussion with your trainers and supervisor (as highlighted in Figure 2.1) as part of the overall assessment of your readiness to commence work with clients at this point in time.

Reflecting on therapeutic practice and skills

Formal development of therapeutic practice takes numerous forms within training. This may include observation by peers and/or tutors, review of recorded sessions, role plays as well as discussion of specific skills, techniques and dynamics and the likely impact of each within the therapeutic relationship and/or process. Practically, you are likely to take on the role of therapist with one of your peers acting as a client together with one or more observers. However, we do not want to disregard the considerable amount of experience of relating to others you have accumulated prior to entering the training context. This means that you will have already developed a 'skills base', some of which will undoubtedly be transferable into the field of counselling and psychotherapy. Identifying what is transferable and acquiring new skills and techniques to support you in preparing for working in placement, all constitutes part of what McLeod refers to as *mastery of technique*, 'knowledge of when and how to carry out specific interventions, ability to assess effectiveness of interventions, understanding of rationale behind techniques and possession of a sufficiently wide repertoire of interventions or methods' (2009: 613). There is acknowledgement within the accreditation and registration processes of professional bodies such as BACP and UKCP that development of this repertoire will take place both within the training context and through 'live' on-the-job experience. Considerable weighting is afforded to each of these components; for example, the BACP, in their accreditation criteria, specify a requirement for both 450 'tutor contact hours' and 450 hours of face-to-face client experience. As client work is supervised this increases the time obligation in regard to your on-the-job training, and thus the placement component of a trainee's experience can be seen as a major factor intrinsic to the success of formal training.

> McLeod defines 'skill' within the therapeutic context as referring 'to a sequence of counsellor actions or behaviours carried out in response to client actions or behaviours. Implicit in the idea of skill is an assumption that it makes sense to break down the role of counsellor into discrete actions or behaviours' (2009: 622–3). Some skills identified by McLeod are: attending behaviour, open and closed questions, paraphrasing and summarising, reflecting feeling, and meaning and confrontation.

Therefore, we are proposing that development of aptitude as a therapist in this respect is composed of three elements:

1. therapeutic practice within the training context
2. accumulated life experiences with regard to relating to others
3. on-the-job experience.

We recommend holding these three components in mind when assessing your own readiness to engage in the placement experience as it may be useful to reflect upon the development of your therapeutic practice from two different, yet complementary perspectives:

- Reflection from a reductionist perspective will enable you to think about which skills and techniques you have learned about and applied so far, and which you need to develop.
- Reflection from a holistic perspective will support you to consider your wider knowledge and experience of relating in order to think about the development of your therapeutic practice.

Mearns (1997) highlights the overlapping nature of these standpoints. For example, it is impossible to think about how a particular skill or technique is being used without thinking about its impact on the relationship overall. Furthermore, if you identify any habitual ways of relating influencing your therapeutic style, it may be of benefit to explore this with other supportive professionals. Although there is no way to anticipate what your early client experience will be like, we hope that this will give you sufficient grounding in your own competence as you start to reflect on the prospect of seeing clients in placement.

I had an interesting conversation with a fellow trainee who had recently started their placement which gave me lots of food for thought. One area that stood out to me was related to the relatively artificial nature of skills practice within the training context. Although I agree that observed practice in training is beneficial, when working with peers there is a shared language and understanding developing. This means that along with the fact that we know each other it makes for a very different experience than I can expect in placement. I anticipate that sitting in front of a 'real' client is going to be a very steep learning curve which I think will test my understanding and applications of the attitudes and skills I am learning about and trying out.

With this in mind, take some time to undertake Activity 2.6 and consider how any learning gained from this activity might usefully enhance your own evaluation of readiness to start the placement search and ultimately undertake practice.

Activity 2.6 Reflection on professional development

Aim

- To facilitate reflection on professional development in order to assess readiness to commence client work.

Background

It is possible to reflect on therapeutic practice in two different but equally important ways:

- Reflection from a reductionist perspective will enable you to think about which skills and techniques you have learned about and applied so far, and which you need to develop.
- Reflection from a holistic perspective will support you to consider your wider knowledge and experience of relating in order to think about the development of your therapeutic practice.

Activity

- Reflect upon the therapeutic practice you have undertaken in the training context in terms of:
    - feedback you have received from peer observers and trainers
    - any personal reflections you have noted (e.g. in your personal training journal or equivalent).
- Using the prompts below as a guide, note your strengths and areas for development from both a reductionist and holistic perspective.

Table 2.1 offers ideas from both reductionist and holistic perspectives.

TABLE 2.1 *Reflection on professional development*

Reflection from a reductionist perspective	Reflection from a holistic perspective
- What skills and techniques have I used so far? - What feedback have I received about my use of these? - What are my personal reflections about the skills and techniques I do well, and those I need to develop? - How might I work on the skills and techniques needing development? - Are there any skills and techniques I have learned about but have not yet had a chance to use in practice? If so, how might I develop an appropriate level of competence in order that these might be used in client work?	- What is my experience so far in the role of therapist? - What feedback have I received about myself in the role of therapist, and how does this link to my style of relating overall? - What are my strengths, and what have been the highlights of this process? - What have I learned about my own processes, and areas I need to attend to? (This might include noticing strong responses to particular elements of client material or identification of repeated patterns of interaction.) - How might I work on those areas I currently identify as needing attention?

- Reflect on your responses in relation to your readiness to commence placement. How might you utilise your self-knowledge in this instance? Are there areas you need to address? What might you consider further with support from peers, tutors, supervisors?

A PDF version of this activity is available to download from https://study.sagepub.com/oldaleandcooke

Feedback from my peers suggested that I was asking lots of questions within skills practice. Whilst this was eliciting some interesting information from my 'client', the overall impact was sometimes that they felt misunderstood in some of the detail of what they were trying to convey. This has led me to start actively working on the skills of reflection, paraphrasing and summarising in continuing skills work. My trainer has indicated that far from preventing me from being ready to undertake placement, identifying and working on these areas is enhancing my skills base. Also, he suggested that I could use this as an example to illustrate my awareness and attention to ongoing development in the application and interview process.

I had not been aware, until it was pointed out in tutor feedback during a specific session, that I had completely missed an important component of what the 'client' was trying to convey. The 'client' confirmed that this was the case and that they had perceived me to lack warmth and genuine presence. Although this feedback was difficult to receive, I realised that my ability to be consistently in the relationship was compromised and that this was related to painful experiences in my own life … which I tend to avoid addressing. As this is likely to repeatedly impact upon my availability and warmth, I have decided to discuss this with my supervisor as I'm wondering whether I should delay moving into placement. I'm not sure I'm ready! Also I am going to discuss this in my next therapy session as I really want to be able to engage and remain present with others, including any future clients I may work with.

We acknowledge that each trainee, placement experience and client is unique and therefore you will apply the expertise that you have accumulated and work on your areas for development in different ways. The reflective points at the end of this chapter will support you in identifying how you may use this information as part of an assessment of your overall readiness as well as to personally apply what you have learned to the placement search and application process and the placement endeavour itself.

Practical considerations

Training as a therapist is a highly demanding endeavour. Only in extremely rare circumstances is psychotherapy or counselling training undertaken in isolation of other personal or professional roles. Even those undertaking full-time courses will likely have family and/or work commitments competing for their time and attention. Throughout the duration of your training you will be focused on your academic studies and development (both personal and professional); as a consequence you are probably changing as an individual. As a result of this focus and change, many trainees find that psychotherapy training presents some degree of challenge for those closest to them. For instance, in all likelihood you will find that your training has an increased practical impact on your family whilst undertaking your placement(s). Most trainee therapists find that taking time to discuss aspects of this with family members, in advance of beginning their placement and throughout their training, ensures a greater degree of understanding and continued support.

Preparing for Placement: Personal, Theoretical and Ethical Considerations

My family have supported me from the beginning of my training and are proud that I am achieving my goals. However, I have far less free time to spend with them and find I really need to be organised to keep on top of everything. I was worried about how to include a placement in my schedule and began to feel concerned that I might not be able to cope and that my family might want me to quit training if more demands were made on my time. My trainer encouraged me to discuss this with my family. I'm so glad I did this as we were able to put a plan together which meant that I had some extra support, both practically and emotionally. I would say to any new student getting ready to begin placement – seek the support of your significant others early on in the process, try to work together to identify ways to manage the demands of training alongside other aspects of your life circumstances. It's only short term and the long term rewards are brilliant!

Some careful planning and practical consideration can contribute towards success in early and ongoing placement experience. Identifying and keeping key practical factors in mind can enable you to make decisions; for example, regarding the location of your placement search and the number of clients you can feasibly see in the time you have available. Of course, considerations such as these will be negotiated with the placement provider and your supervisor; however, it is useful to identify any potential practical limitations from the outset as this will ensure that your negotiations are well informed and that, among other things, you are not initially overwhelmed. It is also vital to remember that the placement is not a self-contained activity. Alongside your commencement of client work is the requirement to begin supervision (which will be discussed initially in Chapter 3). You will need to ensure that you set aside sufficient time to reflect on your practice, how you best manage the client relationships and how these impact you.

As mentioned in Chapter 1, there is far more to be gained from placement experience than simple accumulation of client hours towards the requirements of your qualification. You may learn about various aspects of the organisation, client group and sector through engagement with tasks other than counselling, which will in turn support you in the therapist role. Organisations will vary in their requirements of trainees in this respect. Although engaging in a specific number of hours of activities of this nature is no longer a requirement of BACP accredited courses, it is worth referring to their definition of the types of activity deemed worthwhile, namely: 'clerical duties; attending team meetings; case management conference; reading literature, policies and procedures; skills practice; structured training; observation, assisting, mentoring or job shadowing' (BACP, 2009: 12). In your overall consideration of the time you have available it is worth balancing the benefits of these wider activities with the predicted impact on your overall schedule and work–life balance.

In addition to the above-mentioned factors, it is probable that you will identify and need to address a variety of practical concerns unique to your personal circumstances. Below we have listed some examples of further areas for consideration, together with some specific trainee comments which might support you in considering your own personal situation when preparing to search for your placement and commence practice:

- any financial implications (e.g. supervision fees; any placement provider costs; travel and/or parking)
- travel time to and from placement; supervision; personal therapy
- study time
- keeping in touch with fellow trainees
- social life
- self-care (including, although not exclusively limited to, personal therapy).

As a wheelchair user, it is important to me that the counselling rooms in my placement organisation are accessible.

I am the parent of two small children, and on a tight financial budget. I cannot afford to pay out for any more childcare than I am already. This means I need to finish my placement in time to pick up the children from school.

I live in a remote rural community and therefore driving has to be my means of getting to my placement. Free or low-cost parking is near the top of my priority list.

Your training provider, placement organisation, supervisor and fellow trainees will probably have additional suggestions about areas to include within your reflections. In addition, we hope Activity 2.7 will provide a basis for you to set realistic expectations of yourself, and support you to make informed decisions about how much time you have available and the ways in which you might manage the components central to your personal circumstances.

Activity 2.7 Pre-placement practical considerations

Aims

- To support identification and reflection on key practical considerations likely to impact you when undertaking a placement and its related activities.

Background

Counselling and psychotherapy training is rarely undertaken in isolation of other roles. Additionally, commencing placement constitutes undertaking a number of related activities, professional and practical, which will place demands upon time (e.g. preparation for supervision; travel to and from the placement venue; attending agency meetings).

Activity

- Take some time to reflect upon your current commitments. You may wish to use the timetable in Table 2.2 to map out what a 'typical' week looks like for you. Include:

    o home/family commitments
    o work commitments
    o study/training commitments (reading and research, assignments and writing, personal therapy, etc.)

TABLE 2.2 Reflections on ethics – weekly schedule

	Monday	Tuesday	Wednesday	Thursday	Friday	Saturday	Sunday
Morning							
Afternoon							
Evening							

(Continued)

(Continued)
- o self-care/hobbies/pastimes
- o anything else important to you.

- What thoughts and feelings come up for you as you reflect on the overall picture?
- How will a placement and related activities fit within the current picture?
- What, if anything, will you need to change? How might you go about achieving any changes in order to ensure you are prepared to begin placement from a practical perspective?

A PDF version of this activity is available to download from https://study.sagepub.com/oldaleandcooke

Chapter summary and ongoing reflections

This chapter has considered the relevance of pre-placement reflection in regard to your motivations to practise as a therapist, the philosophical, theoretical and ethical dimensions of your understanding, your personal and professional development as well as your practical circumstances. You have had opportunity to undertake a number of activities and we hope that this will support you in:

- managing potential anxiety and sense of vulnerability as you strive to present a positive impression of yourself to potential placement providers within initial enquiries, your application and interview (see Chapter 4)
- identifying your learning objectives and meeting these in practice.

We hope that all of these points have enabled you to consider whether you are ready at this moment in time to begin the search for a placement. Chapter 3 considers the training provider and wider professional requirements that you will need to factor into your preparation as you move into the actual search and application process considered in Chapter 4. Before moving on to these chapters you may wish to reflect upon key aspects of your learning. We have therefore provided a number of points for consideration below, based on the reflective learning cycle discussed in the Introduction. We hope that this assists you to identify action points that you may personally take forward.

1. Record your thoughts and feelings as you come to the end of the chapter, with specific reference to the activities you have undertaken.
2. List one or two main areas of learning.
3. List any points of action or further enquiry that you will undertake in relation to assessing your own readiness to practise and preparation for placement.
4. Set a deadline for yourself to undertake any actions you have highlighted in point 3 above.

Further reading

For those interested in further considering their personal motivations for training as a therapist, two texts stand out. First of all Sofie Bager-Charleson's (2010) book *Why Therapists Choose to Become Therapists: A Practice-based Enquiry* and second, *A Curious Calling: Unconscious Motivations for Practicing Psychotherapy* by Michael Sussman (2007). The philosophical and theoretical understanding activity in this chapter was in part influenced by ideas from McLeod's (2009) *Introduction to Counselling*, specifically Chapter 3, and you may find that chapter useful for further reflection in regard to this area. Tim Bond's book *Standards and Ethics for Counselling in Action* (2010) provides an excellent introduction to ethics in practice. *Counselling, Psychotherapy and the Law* by Peter Jenkins (2007) gives detailed ideas about how legislation is applicable to the role of the therapist. Trainees who are considering readiness and who are student members of BACP may find the *Am I Fit to Practise as a Counsellor* information sheet a useful supplement to the activities in this chapter.

References

Asay, T.P. and Lambert, M.J. (1999) 'The empirical case for the common factors in therapy: quantitative findings', in M. Hubble, B.L. Duncan and S.D. Miller (eds), *The Heart and Soul of Change: What Works in Therapy*. Washington, DC: American Psychological Association, pp. 33–55.

Bager-Charleson, S. (2010) *Why Therapists Choose to Become Therapists: A Practice-based Enquiry*. London: Karnac.

Bond, T. (2010) *Standards and Ethics for Counselling in Action*. London: Sage.

British Association for Counselling and Psychotherapy (BACP) (2009) *Accreditation of Training Courses*. Lutterworth: British Association for Counselling and Psychotherapy.

British Association for Counselling and Psychotherapy (BACP) (2013) *Ethical Framework for Good Practice in Counselling and Psychotherapy*. Available at: www.bacp.co.uk/admin/structure/files/pdf/9479_ethical%20framework%20jan2013.pdf (accessed 23.03.14).

Feltham, C. and Dryden, W. (1993) *Dictionary of Counselling*. London: Whurr.

HM Government (2004) *The Children Act*. London: Stationery Office.

HM Government (2005) *The Prevention of Terrorism Act*. London: Stationery Office.

HM Government (2010) *The Equality Act*. London: Stationery Office.

Jenkins, P. (2007) *Counselling, Psychotherapy and the Law*. London: Sage.

Kolb, D.A. (1984) *Experiential Learning: Experience as the Source of Learning and Development*. Upper Saddle River, NJ: Prentice Hall.

McLeod, J. (2009) *Introduction to Counselling*, 4th edn. Maidenhead: Open University Press.

Mearns, D. (1997) *Person-Centred Counselling Training*. London: Sage.
Sussman, M.B. (2007) *A Curious Calling: Unconscious Motivations for Practicing Psychotherapy*. Plymouth: Jason Aronson.
Thorne, B. and Dryden, W. (1991) *Training and Supervision for Counselling in Action*. London: Sage.
Tosey, P. and Gregory, J. (2002) *Dictionary of Personal Development*. London: Whurr.
United Kingdom Council for Psychotherapy (UKCP) (2009) *Ethical Principles and Code of Conduct*. Available at: www.psychotherapy.org.uk/code_of_ethics.html (accessed 06.09.11).
Whitton, E. (2003) *Humanistic Approach to Psychotherapy*. London: Whurr.

Three

Before You Start: Training Provider and Wider Professional Considerations

This chapter will:

- Invite consideration of the requirements of your training provider in regard to the placement endeavour whilst supporting reflection in relation to:
  - the relationship between fitness, competence and readiness to practise and how this is assessed
  - accrual of client and supervision hours
  - placement and client specific factors
  - the academic component including video/audio-recording and writing about work in placement
  - selection of an appropriate supervisor and pre-placement use of supervision
  - contractual issues
  - wider professional issues.

The previous chapter considered several aspects of your readiness to begin working with clients, with specific attention to the importance of practitioner fitness and competence. The reflective activities in relation to areas such as theory, ethics, personal development and practical circumstances were designed to support you in considering the implications of these areas in preparation for the placement search and undertaking. We hope that this together with collaborative support from other professionals (for instance, your training provider) will play a part in the continual decision-making process about whether you are currently ready to start in placement (and what needs to change or develop if you assess yourself not to be in a position to commence your search). This chapter invites you to find out, or re-familiarise yourself with, further factors that need to be taken into account before you commence the placement search. These include the specific requirements of your training provider and any aligned professional bodies. We introduce the idea of supervision as an essential component to support your decisions about readiness, the placement search and your work within the placement itself, together with your career-long practice as a therapist.

> I'm keen to put what I've been learning into action and although I feel excited about this, it's really daunting to think about all the things that are needed by my training institution and the profession. Right now this looks like a huge mountain to climb with me a tiny figure at the bottom in the foothills.

We acknowledge that being at the point in your training at which the prospect of securing a placement is imminent can be both an exciting yet daunting time. Embarking on a process of preparation before continuing on the journey of gaining professional experience and recognition will not make the climb any less steep. However, it will ensure (as far as possible) that you have the tools you need for the ascent and (looking to the reflective activities in this chapter and beyond) that you have sufficient points at which to pause and take stock of your progress as well as plan next steps. The specifics of this chapter attempt to chart significant aspects of the terrain including consideration of:

> Since practice requirements are constantly reviewed to ensure their continued relevance, you should periodically check with accrediting bodies such as BACP and UKCP to keep up to date with competency requirements. Ethical Codes and Frameworks are a good place to start. Additionally, good practice guidelines for training such as BACP's (2012) 'gold book' *Accreditation of Training Courses including the Core Curriculum* provide key information on the standards for their accredited training courses and a useful resource for the trainee wishing to keep up to date with what is expected of them.

- key areas to support you in the process of assessment of your readiness, thereby ensuring that you are adequately prepared for the additional professional and academic commitments that accompany the commencement of your work with clients
- training provider and relevant professional body requirements, which will assist you in the collaborative process of selecting an appropriate placement and supervisor.

Attention to these requirements will enable all parties to fully engage in the contracts and agreements made in regard to the placement activity. Additionally, this knowledge is vital in ensuring the ethical use of practice-based material in your academic work and will again be relevant to contractual agreements with supervisors, placement providers and clients.

We will consider how training provider and professional body requirements are likely to impact upon you as you commence the placement search and embark upon your journey into practice. Undertaking the activities in this chapter will enable you to gather important information in a form that is easy to reference at a glance. As such it would be useful to locate and have with you your training course handbook and/or other materials relating to the academic and professional requirements set out by your training provider. We hope that this will be useful as you begin your placement search and application process (the latter being discussed in Chapter 4).

… Before You Start: Training Provider and Wider Professional Considerations

Training provider requirements

It is widely accepted within the profession of counselling and psychotherapy that the organisation providing training, together with the supervisor, has a role as a 'gatekeeper to the profession'. It is their professional responsibility to consider whether, ultimately, the person in training is sufficiently competent to begin working with clients. Assuming this competence is evident, and the trainee is also fit to practise (according to the definitions of competence and fitness provided in the Introduction, and expanded in Chapter 2), progression will occur and eventually qualification will be awarded.

The nature of this training and the development of courses accredited by awarding bodies, education providers and professional organisations necessitate a blending of the academic, personal and professional. Thus, the evaluation of whether a person should be awarded a counselling or psychotherapy qualification (and ultimately, secure professional registration and/or accreditation) will depend upon assessment of all of these factors. This section considers some common academic and professional requirements in relation to the pending placement search.

When referring to your course information or handbook you will probably find that requirements are broken down into a number of components designed to assess different areas of competence, with some necessary areas of overlap:

> Feltham and Dryden define a **transcript** as 'a written account of a counselling session using actual (verbatim) dialogue ... recordings are requested on some training courses for assessment; the actual dialogue may be accompanied by a commentary on the counsellor's intentions, his views on how well he intervened and what alternative interventions he might have made' (1993: 197). Transcripts and similar pieces of work may also be called **process reports**. In contrast, a **case study** uses the therapist's cumulative knowledge of a single therapeutic relationship to demonstrate their effectiveness, management of professional and ethical issues, appropriateness of interventions and to critique their practice overall (McLeod, 2010). Thus, both pieces of work completed as part of the training endeavour will assess similar components of counsellor competency but using a different format.

- Academic requirements may include essays, presentations and different ways of writing about clinical practice including, but not limited to, case studies and transcripts of your work with your analysis of content and process (sometimes called 'process reports'). Within these pieces of work you may also be asked to demonstrate how you draw on the body of research knowledge to inform and critique your practice. You may even be asked to undertake an independent piece of research in the field.
- Practice-based requirements include demonstrating knowledge, understanding and application of the requirements of your ethical codes/framework. It will also include accruing an agreed number of hours of supervised work with clients and

evidencing your competence in this area. This might be shown through the academic work mentioned above and/or through written reports supplied by your supervisor and/or placement provider; it may also be assessed through observations in the training context with opportunity for input from tutor and peers.
- Personal development requirements might include completion of a certain number of hours of personal therapy and participation in other developmental activities such as a personal development group. This may be assessed through, for example, self, peer and tutor reports, journal writing or again through academic writing.

You may find that the areas assessed and pieces of work required to evidence your learning and development are given different names according to your training provider. Having said this, common themes are likely to be evident, each of which will impact on how and when you undertake the placement search and your practice therein. Starting with practice-based requirements, we consider how your training provider might assess your readiness to start client work, with specific reference to competence and fitness. From this we then explore the 'numbers' side of things – how many hours you actually need to gain as part of working towards qualification and/or professional recognition. We then take a look at the place of supervision, giving an overview of its purpose and how you might select an appropriate supervisor. Within this we examine ways in which supervision might be utilised in preparing for placement and again look at 'numbers' and required ratios of supervision to client work. Turning our attention to academic requirements, we highlight ways in which you might approach and undertake recording and writing about clinical practice, ensuring this endeavour is ethically grounded. Finally we consider how the relationship between yourself, your training provider, placement and supervisor is summarised contractually to provide a basis for your working relationship.

Assessment of readiness

> If assessment of readiness were expressed as an equation, it might look like 'Competence + Fitness = Readiness'.

It is likely that your training provider will have both informal and formal processes which allow them to assess your readiness to start work with clients. Referring to our previous definitions of competence and fitness, you will likely be assessed on your competence and knowledge in various areas, your personal development and circumstances.

Assessment of this kind will probably include a combination of the following:

- explicit consideration of your competence and fitness to practise as it has been demonstrated within training so far
- providing a written rationale, essay, report or giving a presentation about your readiness, which might include theoretical, professional/ethical and personal developmental components
- a formal or informal observation of your practice by tutors and peers
- feedback on your readiness from tutors and peers.

You have already started to assess your own readiness through the activities in Chapter 2. In addition, this process will have begun informally within your training,

Before You Start: Training Provider and Wider Professional Considerations

for instance, via observed skills sessions and/or formal assessment of written work. Therefore, you can see that readiness is of concern whether your training provider uses regular modes of assessment or a specific assessment at the end of a particular training period.

As a trainer it is import to me that I get a sense of whether a trainee is ready to start working with clients even before they undertake the formal observation which is undertaken at the end of the first year. I use a range of information to make this ongoing assessment. This includes observing practice sessions (including discussion of feedback, theoretical, ethical, personal and professional issues arising) and drawing on my observations and experience of a trainee's relational attitudes and capabilities across the different aspects of the training. I also check in regularly with trainees about their personal circumstances and how this is supportive (or otherwise) of the current training, including the placement search. This means I can be as sure as possible that the individual is ready, and that their expectations are managed by explicit discussion of strengths and areas for development.

To support you in considering the groundwork you have done so far, you may wish to undertake Activity 3.1. This looks at what has gone before in terms of the preparation and work you have undertaken and relates this to any formal assessment process which might be in place.

Activity 3.1 Training provider assessment of readiness

Aim

- To support you in clarifying how your training provider will assess your readiness to commence client work in placement.
- To facilitate you to consider how you might use feedback related to common themes in preparation for any assessment of readiness your training provider undertakes.

Background

Assessment of readiness takes many forms and varies from training provider to training provider. Common themes are discussed in Chapter 2, and you have already started to reflect on these. Early training is about assessing these areas overall and there may or may not be a formal readiness process; even if there is not, the learning and feedback can support you as part of your reflection on readiness to start work with clients.

Activity

Using the experience from your training course, its associated handbook and any other relevant materials, complete the grid in Table 3.1 stating how each

(Continued)

(Continued)

TABLE 3.1 Assessment of readiness grid

AREA ASSESSED	PREVIOUS ASSESSMENTS (e.g. written work, observations, journals, peer and tutor assessments)	FORMAL READINESS ASSESSMENT
Understanding of Philosophical and Theoretical Underpinnings of the Approach		
Ethical Understanding		
Therapeutic Skills and Attitudes		
Personal Development/Soundness		

Before You Start: Training Provider and Wider Professional Considerations

> component listed has been or will be assessed as part of your overall assessment of readiness to start work in placement. Give as much detail as possible.
>
> Reflecting on the above, think about how the learning and feedback received from previous assessments might support you in any formal assessment of readiness undertaken by your training provider. Make note of your responses in your training journal (or equivalent).
>
> *A PDF version of this activity is available to download from https://study.sagepub.com/oldaleandcooke*

You might want to revisit your responses to the activities undertaken throughout the previous chapter and consider how these could support your preparation for any assessment of readiness carried out by your training provider. For example, you might think about how your responses to Activity 2.6 (reflection on professional development) support you to prepare for an observed session if this forms part of the assessment of readiness.

In my first year of training everything was very new. I was learning to relate to a new group of people and trying to think about how I related to some complex philosophical, theoretical and ethical ideas. I found that the assignments set by my training provider supported me to reflect on my readiness to practise – sometimes without realising it! For example, the marking criteria for written work incorporated a component of how ideas might apply in practice and asked us to use examples from training to support these points. The whole process of interacting with a group of people ethically and in line with the theoretical model of the training means that examples were there to be used and explored. This meant that in the dynamic interactions of the group, experience was being gained, applied and written about. As I now come to reflect on this experience I can see that it has supported me to arrive at a place where I am ready to start work with clients, and that both I and my trainers have been evaluating this along the way.

Preparing for self-assessment

You have already begun the process of assessing your own readiness in Chapter 2 where you considered:

- understanding of the philosophical and theoretical underpinnings of your chosen therapeutic approach
- willingness to engage with ethics as a process
- your development thus far on your training
- your personal situation and the practicalities of undertaking a placement.

We hope that this has given you the opportunity to reflect upon whether you are ready to commence client work at this point in time. For some trainees, reflection can lead to the conclusion that they are not currently in a position to search for and commence placement. There are a number of possible reasons why this might be the case, including but not limited to:

- identification of key theoretical, ethical or developmental issues which require further attention, for example:
  - the need to develop further expertise in skills and techniques used by the core model of your training
  - the need to acquire more grounding in core theoretical and ethical knowledge
  - the requirement to work on a particular process or developmental issue which, if unaddressed, may detrimentally impact on the wellbeing of the client, therapist or both
- a need for a change in practical circumstances (such as a change in working hours)
- a major life event (such as bereavement, divorce, change in accommodation or job, becoming a parent or carer).

I was in the unfortunate position of being made redundant halfway through the first year of training. This impacted my life and possibilities for ongoing training in a number of ways. Whilst I thought, at first, that the extra time would be invaluable to me in that it would provide a space in which to see clients, it quickly became apparent that I would be unable to afford the following year's course fees and allow a reasonable level of subsistence for my family. Alongside that, I realised in personal therapy that the loss of my job had triggered an emotional response to an earlier sudden loss in my life. I was suddenly in a position where I was neither practically nor emotionally able to say that I was ready to start seeing clients. I took a year out and managed to secure a part-time job which allowed a reasonable level of income, contributing to course fees and a reasonable level of family life, yet gave sufficient time in the week for me to undertake the placement which I have now secured. Looking back, the decision to defer was really hard, but the foundations I was able to put in place in terms of practicalities and work in personal therapy meant I was more ready than ever to commence work with clients when I returned.

The above example illustrates the complex interplay between personal and professional factors. Often practical circumstances trigger emotional responses which need exploration. We are not suggesting that all those who have identified with aspects of the above will not be ready to commence practice. However, we are suggesting that if the above or something similar applies, it would be beneficial to discuss with your tutors and others supporting you in order to ascertain how factors might impact should you commence work with clients. Equally you may wish to discuss the implications of delaying the placement search (e.g. delaying may mean that hours are not sufficiently accrued in order to proceed to the next stage of your training).

Assessment of fitness and competence is an ongoing endeavour, and it is equally possible that you may identify one of the above or go through a significant life event once you have started in placement. Chapter 6 will discuss the significance of reflexive practice and the decision to continue in placement, seek paid work or indeed the possibility of undertaking both.

Preparing for assessment by others

The idea of formal (and indeed informal) assessment can provoke an anxiety response. This response is natural. As mentioned previously, assessment occurs on an ongoing basis in counselling and psychotherapy training programmes and usually includes elements of self, peer and tutor assessment. Individual responses to assessment will vary and may differ according to who is doing the assessing. It is worth noting that the process may also be anxiety provoking for the person doing the assessment!

Our intention here is not to go into an exploration of how various therapeutic models might see the roots of anxiety, although no doubt that would be an interesting endeavour. Instead, we aim to highlight the reality of anxiety as one possible response when undertaking an assessment process. In addition, we are keen to invite evaluation in regard to how it uniquely manifests for you as well as to discuss some ways in which you might manage the impact of the response. In our view, this exercise will be useful not only here, but we intend to refer to it again within Chapter 4 when we discuss the placement application and interview process.

Activity 3.2 enables you to consider your personal responses to assessments or other anxiety provoking situations. In this way it invites consideration of both positive and less constructive coping strategies, taking inspiration from the ABCDE model (Ellis, 1994) used in rational emotional behavioural therapy – a variant of cognitive behavioural therapy.

> The ABCDE model was devised by Albert Ellis as a way for individuals to overcome what he saw as 'irrational' belief systems. Although different models may critique the notion of 'irrational' according to their underlying philosophical assumptions, the basis of the ABCDE model can be of help in unpacking the responses related to anxiety provoking events and devising alternative ways of responding:
>
> A = Activating event (the trigger)
> B = Beliefs (Ellis believed that irrational beliefs are problematic and cause and lead to consequences)
> C = Consequences (thoughts and feelings which may be a barrier to taking constructive action in the circumstances)
> D = Disputation (disputing the belief and finding alternative ways of thinking, feeling and responding)
> E = Experimentation/Evaluation (trying out alternative ways of thinking, feeling and responding as well as assessing the success of this).

We have selected Ellis's ABCDE model as it may provide a useful practical model to address your anxieties. If other issues are highlighted in the process of undertaking the activity we would suggest you talk this through with a supportive other, such as your tutor or personal therapist.

Activity 3.2 Responses to being assessed

Activity Aim

- To support the identification of responses to being assessed
- To facilitate consideration of coping strategies evoked in regard to being assessed

Background

This activity is adapted from the ABCDE model utilised within some in Cognitive Behavioural Approaches to Therapy. We have selected this as it may provide a

(Continued)

(Continued)

TABLE 3.2 *Responses to being assessed*

Make note of your responses with particular attention to your thoughts and beliefs about the situation.

What do you imagine might be the consequences of these beliefs when being assessed in regard to:

Thoughts? | Feelings? | Barriers to constructive action?

How might I challenge any beliefs likely to hinder my ability to effectively engage in a readiness to begin placement assessment process?

What strategies have I used previously to manage my responses to being assessed?

Useful strategies? | Hindering strategies?

What can I do to support the development of constructive strategies and prevent myself from using hindering strategies when being assessed?

Develop | Prevent

useful practical model for you to address your anxieties although if other issues are highlighted in the process of undertaking the activity we would suggest you talk this through with a supportive other such as your tutor, or therapist.

Activity

Imagine you are about to undertake an observed practice session which forms part of your training providers assessment of your competence and ultimately your readiness to begin placement (A = activating event). Next, consider the prompts in the table below and complete relevant sections with your responses.

Finally, you might find it useful to return to this activity replacing the activating event with other imagined scenarios; for instance, attending placement interviews or preparing to see your first client or to meet your supervisor for the first time.

A PDF version of this activity is available to download from https://study.sagepub.com/oldaleandcooke

The following vignettes show how other trainees managed and learned from assessment anxiety in their individual ways.

I found that some of the techniques I have used in meditation and mindfulness have really helped me to cope with the anxiety around assessments. I learned in meditation that naming an aspect of my experience can help me to own it, and notice that it is part of a multiplicity of experiences that are happening for me at the time. So depending on the appropriateness of the situation, I might 'out loud' my nervousness or acknowledge it to myself. Doing this in my assessed session enabled me to move on to other aspects of experience (my sense of excitement about the imminent placement search, the way that my 'client' was sitting and seeming fidgety, even the more basic sense of the uncomfortable temperature in the room which I was able to rectify). I found this really useful in allowing my anxiety to naturally dissipate in the overall spectrum of experience. In doing so I also realised my experience of being assessed was far less anxiety provoking than I had imagined!

My strategy to cope with nervousness is to talk … and talk … and talk some more! You can imagine that this is not very helpful in an assessed counselling situation where the focus is meant to be on the client! Unfortunately this was a feature of my readiness-to-practise observed session. I thought that 'was it', that I would be told I was not ready to start work with clients. In fact, I found that my observers and tutors were able to look beyond my nervousness to some of the skills and qualities I had demonstrated well. Although I was asked to explore my tendency to over-talk in early supervision, I was thrilled to pass my assessment and am now seeking a placement.

Ensuring that you are prepared

As well as the steps outlined above, there are a number of practical things you can do to ensure that you are prepared on the day of any formal assessment:

- check in your training course handbook to ensure that you are familiar with the assessment criteria
- ensure that you have brought along everything you need (e.g. if you have prepared a presentation about your readiness, check whether you are required to provide handouts for the assessors and, if so, how many people will be in the assessment group. Also, if the session is being audio or video recorded, who provides the equipment and ensures that it is working beforehand?)
- make sure you know where your assessment is being undertaken
- arrive on time (or early!) for the start of the session. Even small delays can add to your own anxiety and that of other trainees, as well as causing considerable disruption to the assessment schedule.

Attending to the above means it is more likely that you, your trainers and peer assessors in the group will be as relaxed as possible. Remember that your peers may also be anxious as they may in turn be waiting to be assessed. Tutors may be concerned about the process running smoothly and fitting everyone into the scheduled timetable. Helping yourself means you are more likely to be focused on your 'client'. Supporting others means they are more likely to be focused enough to give you good-quality feedback.

Table 3.3 offers a form that may be used to gather feedback from your assessment session.

It should be noted that this is an example only and you should make sure you are familiar with the feedback form used by your training provider. In this example, concrete feedback is invited from the observer(s) about the skills and qualities of the therapist as demonstrated in the session. In addition, space is given for areas of theoretical and ethical discussion.

Giving feedback

It is worthwhile considering that feedback involves activity from both observer(s) and the observed party. We would, therefore, like to spend a moment considering what it means to provide useful feedback. Essentially, it is important that any feedback offered contributes to the development of the person you are observing, whether they are successful or otherwise.

From the outset it is useful to acknowledge that the process of observation and the giving of feedback is a highly subjective process. Both you and your peers will be developing your own unique way of being with clients. What works for you may well not work for another person. And what works for one client may not work well for another. As an observer you are in a unique position of having a perspective on the session without being (directly) involved in the therapeutic process. For this reason we suggest the following:

- offer feedback as a personally owned point of observation with a concrete example, such as 'When you shook your head early in the session it seemed **to me** as though you were disagreeing with your client'
- allow the person being observed the opportunity to discuss the point being raised. Depending on time available you might consider openly inviting discussion, for example 'I am interested in what was going on for you when you were shaking your head, and how you saw this impacting on the session'

TABLE 3.3 *Observed readiness to practise session example feedback form*

Name of trainee therapist	
Name of observer	
Date of observation	|//
Skills and qualities demonstrated well (provide specific examples)	
Skills and qualities for development (provide specific examples)	
Theoretical observations for discussion	
Ethical observations for discussion	
Further comments and feedback (if applicable)	

Pass: Yes/No (delete as applicable)

- be open to responses which might involve practical discussion of skills or more personal developmental material
- handle any discussion of the therapist's responses to 'client' material sensitively; avoiding reopening or analysing the content or process (for both the therapist and 'client'), particularly if this has involved the sharing of sensitive personal material.

Being the client in an assessed session

Being the 'client' in an assessed session can be as anxiety provoking a position as being the trainee therapist assessed. We wanted to acknowledge the unique position of the client role in the training situation with the following points to keep in mind:

- whether using a role play or your own material, being as natural as possible allows the trainee being assessed to work with realistic responses and processes in the session. This gives the best opportunity for observers to form a sound assessment of the trainee's competence
- when using your own material, consider carefully what to bring so as to ensure your own and the therapist's safety. For example, with material which has only just emerged for you, it may be wise to take this to your own personal therapy, or discuss with a supportive other, before using this in the training context
- different training establishments will have different policies and conventions about how the client can be involved in the feedback process. If in doubt about how this can be handled, your trainer can advise you. We suggest you allow time after the session to reflect and re-ground yourself. This should be the case particularly if personal material has been triggered, or if you need to disengage from the client in a role play so as to not 'carry' the material with you.

Using feedback

When I receive feedback, however constructively it is delivered, a couple of things happen for me and both seem linked to my inner critic. First of all, I find positive feedback really difficult to take in. Secondly, any feedback which is developmental in nature, or points to what I might do differently, puts me in defensive mode so I find it hard to make good use of it.

Whether feedback is positive or constructive (and for best developmental potential it would include aspects of each) it is worth reflecting on what has been said and how you might best use this for your ongoing development. Figure 3.1 suggests a cycle which can be used to develop your own action plan in the light of feedback received. This should encourage constructive action even if, as in the previous vignette, an 'inner critic' is prominent and threatens to sabotage your progress.

The sections of the cycle shown in Figure 3.1 can be explained as follows:

Acknowledgement: This may include stopping to appreciate that the observer has taken the time and effort to feedback to you. Whether you agree or not with the

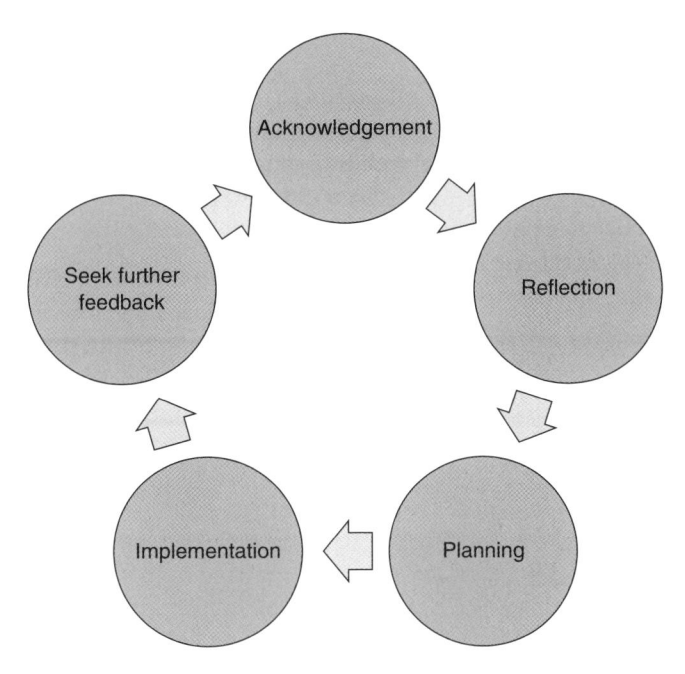

Before You Start: Training Provider and Wider Professional Considerations

FIGURE 3.1 *Responding to feedback*

points they make, we hope that the feedback is given with the best intention and that the feedback will provide a useful basis for reflection.

Reflection: Take time to think about the points raised. Do they match with your experience? Do they match with other feedback you have received? You might decide that the observed behaviour was a one-off, or it was specific to the circumstances. Or you might decide that there is the opportunity for further development.

Planning: If indeed you decide that there is an opportunity for further development, it is useful to make a plan of how you might make concrete actions towards your developmental goal. You could consider setting SMART objectives.

Implementation: Do what you have set as your objective within the timeframe you have allowed for yourself. The implementation phase might include just one action or a number of actions linked to an overall goal.

SMART objectives are often used in business and education to allow action on objectives and thus change to occur in a specific timeframe. The meaning of the SMART acronym is:

- **S**pecific – What exactly is the change you want to make or thing you want to do? Rather than 'I will learn about X' you might say 'I will find a specific book in the library which I know contains information on X'.
- **M**easurable – How will you know when the change has happened? This might look like 'I will have finished Chapter 5 of the book I found in the library'.
- **A**chievable – There is no point setting targets which you are unable to meet, so make sure you have the time and resources to meet your goals.
- **R**ealistic – Similar to achievable, set targets that you do not have to be a superhero to meet, for we are all human with real-life commitments.

> - **T**ime oriented – Take into account what is realistic and achievable; give yourself a specific time for completion, for example 'by next Saturday'.
>
> So the whole SMART objective outlined above might read: 'I will get X book out of the library and read Chapter 5 by next Saturday'.

Seek further feedback: There are a number of ways you might do this. One, which links specifically to the context to which we are referring, might involve seeking further, specific feedback on the next occasion we are observed or assessed.

You will see from Figure 3.1 that the feedback process is continual. Therefore, make space frequently to reflect on feedback and make plans which link to your development. This might occur in tutorial, supervision or peer groups, or in a learning journal if your training course asks you to use one.

Success: drawing on feedback to support the search and application process

If you are successful in the assessment process we would like to offer our congratulations here. It is likely that the feedback you have gained will have much to offer in terms of highlighting strengths and areas for development you might utilise in applications and interviews. Hold on to this material to support you as you embark on your reading of Chapter 4.

Disappointment: learning from feedback to support reassessment

> I did an assessment of readiness last week and my tutor says that I am not ready to start work with clients. I am really disappointed. What can I do?

You may find that an assessment of your readiness indicates that you are not, as yet, ready to commence placement, and it is likely that you will gain specific feedback as to whether the main points of development are around:

- theoretical understanding
- ethical understanding
- personal/developmental
- skills/professional practice.

It is usual to feel disappointed in this instance and taking specific action in regard to feedback using Figure 3.1 may support you to see what you have done well and how far you have already travelled on the road of the trainee therapist. It will also prepare you for your next attempt at assessment of readiness. This might become one of your SMART objectives and you may use your tutor's support to define a timeframe to retake the assessment. In addition, revisiting activities in Chapter 2 may support you.

Maintaining an open and transparent dialogue with your tutors (and supervisor if you have one) will ensure that you can reflect and work on any areas necessary in a productive manner. This will mean that you will be as prepared as possible for reassessment and hopefully in a position to commence the placement search and application process in a timely manner.

Once the readiness process is complete, it is likely that you will seek a supervisor (if you do not already have one) and make steps to secure a placement in which you can accrue supervised client hours. At this point it is worth looking again at the various requirements set. This will mean that you have these in mind and can select and apply for a placement (see Chapter 4) that is likely to meet these needs.

> As an aide-mémoire, the activities that relate to particular areas of competence and fitness are:
>
> - Activity 2.2 – Theoretical understanding
> - Activity 2.4 – Ethical understanding
> - Activity 2.5 – Personal/developmental
> - Activity 2.6 – Skills/professional practice.

Client and supervision hours

Before you start the placement search it is useful to have an awareness of how many hours of supervised client work you need to undertake in order to successfully complete your training course (and future accreditation/registration processes).

It is important to note that we are referring here to the hours you need to accrue to gain the specific qualification offered by your training provider. Although this may allow you to become a full member of a professional body such as the BACP (you may already be a student member), you may need to gain further supervised client hours post-qualification to gain 'accredited' status (in the case of BACP), 'registered' (in the case of UKCP), or to become 'chartered' with a body such as the British Psychological Society (BPS); these issues are addressed in Chapter 6. From 2015, therapists who have not undertaken a BACP accredited course are required to undertake an assessment leading to a Certificate of Proficiency if they wish to remain a BACP member and subsequently apply for accredited status with them.

> We use the term 'supervised client work' to stress that the two activities go hand in hand. Securing a supervisor will be a priority in order that each client hour is supported by the appropriate ratio of supervisory support (which will be explained later in the chapter).

Various training providers will consider a number of criteria to determine the appropriate level of client hours a trainee should accrue to gain qualification, including:

- the level of qualification being sought
- what can realistically be achieved in the duration of training
- the requirements of any bodies accrediting the training, for example the UKCP or BACP.

> The BACP require trainee therapists to undertake supervision at a ratio of 1:8. That is, for every 8 client hours booked, 1 hour of supervision needs to be undertaken. In order to count client hours towards possible accreditation, supervision must be undertaken for at least 1.5 hours per month. The UKCP does not specify a ratio.

On some courses the total requirement might be broken down into annual blocks to illustrate how the amount could be accrued during the training period. For example, if 100 supervised client contact hours are specified and the training course is three years in duration, the first year of training may be spent in preparation for practice with 50 hours being gained during years 2 and 3 of the course. Using these breakdowns as a guide, it is highly probable that you will work closely with both your supervisor and placement provider to agree how these hours will be accrued, considering factors such as how many clients it is appropriate for you to see initially, together with how you will build and manage your caseload.

Further to this, your training provider will specify the ratio of supervision hours you need to undertake for every hour of client work (supervision is discussed in more detail later in this chapter). It is important to remember that supervision hours need to be accrued proportionally and in parallel to the number of client hours undertaken. Training provider requirements normally take into account the minimum required levels of regulatory and accrediting bodies such as the BACP and UKCP. Nevertheless, it is worth familiarising yourself with these requirements to ensure that these are met in the event that you apply for registration or accreditation with a professional body in the future.

Many courses, and indeed trainees, exceed these requirements as it is considered that increased levels of supervision are supportive to the development of theoretical, ethical and professional understanding in the early stages of practice.

The following examples illustrate these points.

Example 1: achieving the required ratio

Tamah is undertaking a BACP accredited training course which requires her to complete 100 hours of face-to-face client work. Her course specifies that she must undertake supervision at a ratio of 1:6 – that is, for every six clients seen she must undertake one hour of supervision.

Tamah has a discussion with her supervisor and placement provider and they decide collaboratively that it would be appropriate for her to start work with three clients. This means that Tamah has three booked client hours per week, or six per fortnight. She therefore needs one hour of supervision per fortnight to stay within her training provider ratios:

>   Fortnightly = 6 (booked) client hours
>   Fortnightly = 1 supervision hour
>   Ratio = 1:6 Supervision to client hours

Example 2: exceeding the ratio

John's course is not BACP accredited. His training provider expects him to undertake 150 hours of client work over two years in order to fulfil qualification requirements. John's training provider has decided to set a ratio of 1:8 supervision to client hours, meaning trainees can work towards BACP accreditation once they qualify if they wish.

John starts work with two clients. On the face of things it seems that he needs only 1 hour per month supervision to support his initial caseload (as he is undertaking 8 client hours per month). However, in order to ensure that he is working towards meeting the BACP criteria for accreditation, the BACP require him to undertake 1.5 hours of supervision per month, meaning he will exceed the 1:8 ratio overall:

> Monthly = 8 (booked) client hours
> Monthly = 1.5 supervision hours (BACP monthly minimum)
> Exceeds BACP 1:8 requirement

There are some further factors to keep in mind when thinking about ratios of supervision to client hours. First and foremost, the ratios set by professional bodies and your training providers are *minimum* requirements. There may be circumstances under which more supervision is needed; for example, in response to a particularly demanding client caseload, or difficult life circumstances. Second, you will need to evidence the ratio of client hours to supervision hours you have undertaken. This is good practice in any case, but is essential as evidence if you are to apply for registration or accreditation with a professional body. Your training provider may provide you with a form to facilitate this. If not it is worth considering how you will record the dates on which client and supervision hours were undertaken in order to evidence your practice. Third, you will notice that we have spoken in terms of client hours *booked* as opposed to clients seen; no shows or 'did not attend' (DNAs) cannot usually be counted towards your total number of supervised client hours. However, it is as important to reflect on the times when clients do not attend sessions as it is to discuss the times when they do. For example, this might highlight important relational, ethical and/or agency policy issues related with non-attendance. In addition, it is important to explore the impact of client non-attendance on yourself as well as the therapeutic relationship in light of the fact that, as a trainee, you are dependent on your client attending their booked sessions to be able to count hours.

At the start of my supervised practice with clients I found it really frustrating when clients did not turn up for booked appointments. The hours requirement seemed like a huge mountain to climb and each DNA felt like a step backwards. I spoke to my supervision group and this was really supportive. My supervisor was able to support me to explore the impact of non-attendance on the therapeutic relationship as well as whether this needed to be discussed explicitly with my clients. It was also useful to pick up practical tips, such as use of appointment cards which acted as an aide-mémoire for my clients.

Accruing sufficient hours for qualification

There may be some circumstances in which you are unable to complete client hours by the end of the formal taught course. For example, your placement may start later than expected or you may need to take a break from practice due to personal circumstances, or due to placement organisational factors such as loss of funding. These instances should of course be discussed with your tutors and supervisor; however, most training providers will have provision for this, allowing some hours to be accrued in an agreed period after the formal taught component of your course has ended. Some trainees may decide to take on more than one placement, time and commitments permitting, in order to gain sufficient hours during the formal taught period.

Placement and client-specific factors

In addition to the client and supervision hours that are necessary to accrue, it is worth considering whether there are any further training provider expectations as part of your pre-placement reflections. For example, if your training is within a specific modality (e.g. person-centred, psychodynamic or cognitive behavioural), you may be required to find a placement in which you are able to practise the modality being studied. Additional expectations may vary, but they are likely to include the placement making provision for the competence level of the trainee in allocation of clients (which may include the need for pre-assessment by a more experienced therapist), providing a safe environment in which to work, and providing adequate placement induction in regard to agency policies and procedures before commencement of work with clients. Chapter 2 also outlined some tasks in addition to the face-to-face client work that may be required by both placement provider and/or training provider. We suggest it would be worth revisiting this to familiarise yourself with possible wider expectations, which will both be an additional commitment and add to your placement experience and development.

Recording and writing about clinical practice

It is likely that your training provider will expect you to make recordings of your client work as well as to write about various aspects of your clinical practice. This fulfils three functions:

- to provide a tool for reflection on your practice within supervision
- to provide evidence for clinical competency and adherence to ethical requirements, thereby ensuring safety in practice
- to enable completion of academic requirements of the award being worked towards.

As mentioned previously, the types of academic work required vary but can include essays, case studies and transcriptions of whole or part sessions in which you may be asked to critically reflect on theoretical, ethical and process aspects of your work. It is therefore essential, when embarking on the placement search, to keep in mind the requirements of your training provider with regard to recording and/or writing about your work, including details in regard to the purpose(s) of this element. This will ensure that you find a placement able to support you in meeting the criteria of your training provider. This may mean that you need to amend or create a separate contract for informed consent with your client to use work in this way. The ethical and practical aspects of this are discussed in Chapter 5.

I thought that I had secured my ideal placement with a client group I really wanted to gain experience with. Unfortunately, at the time of applying, I did not ask whether it would be possible to audio-record work with clients in order to complete a transcript and commentary towards my qualification. I happily accepted the placement when offered to me and it was not until later that I realised I would be unable to gain informed consent to record work with appropriate clients. I really value the experience I had in this placement and of course I accrued a number of hours towards my clinical total, but I wish I had asked at the outset whether recording would be a possibility. Had I done this I could have avoided the additional stress this oversight caused and gained a second placement sooner to facilitate audio-recording to support my professional development and completion of essential pieces of course work.

Informed consent is a term used in counselling and psychotherapy to refer to an agreement from the client that they have been fully informed about and are willing to engage in the process of therapy as it is offered by the particular therapist. This includes the business aspects of therapy such as timing and duration, limits of confidentiality. Of particular interest here is that it will include the fact that the therapist is a trainee, and this brings with it additional components of the relationship, such as a commitment for the trainee to record and write about the work done. Informed consent should be considered carefully with each client to ensure understanding (is the client fully informed?) as well as their ability to give consent (e.g. parental consent may be needed for children and young people, or it may be inappropriate to ask particularly vulnerable clients where cognitive ability is deemed to be impaired). When in doubt always seek advice from your supervisor, training provider or relevant professional body.

Supervision

Supervision is defined by Despenser as 'a formal arrangement for therapists to discuss their work regularly with someone who is experienced in both therapy and supervision' (2011: 1). The way supervision is practised may vary according to the modality and personal style of the supervisor and developmental needs of the individual trainee. In general, however, supervision provides an opportunity to consider both the personal and professional, as illustrated in Figure 3.2.

Work in these domains might take the form of a client being anonymously 'brought' to supervision via a verbal or other (e.g. symbolic) account by the supervisee. The most appropriate ways of working with the client might be discussed in light of the model practised by the trainee therapist and/or the approach taken by the agency.

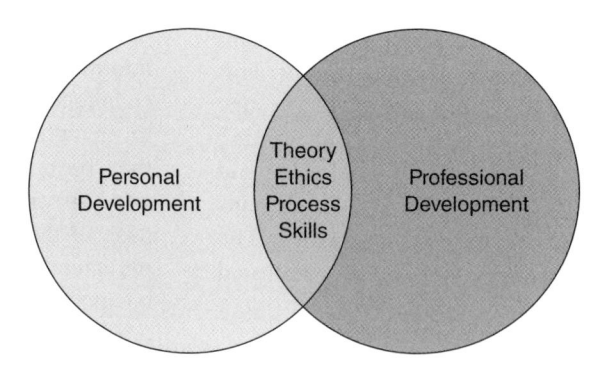

FIGURE 3.2 *Function of supervision*

However, as indicated in Chapter 2, the nature of working as a therapist means that it is impossible to separate your own personal material and processes entirely from the practice of the role. So whilst some of the work of supervision will be in the 'professional development' circle of Figure 3.2, there may well be occasion to consider your personal responses and the ways in which you have been impacted by client material. This may lead to exploration, which is therapeutic in nature and can be continued in personal therapy or by other developmental means. It might equally inform work with an individual client or give insight on a wider issue that is affecting practice. This is in line with a multi-layered model of supervision as outlined by Hawkins and Shohet (2006) where supervision enables therapists to examine both the personal and professional impact of the work they undertake. There are many models of supervision; depending on both the theoretical approach central to your training and the individual style and stance of your supervisor you may find that the following elements are included in varying degrees:

- formal discussion of client 'cases' – sometimes referred to as 'case work' supervision (this is sometimes undertaken with a wider team of therapists and other professionals within an organisation)
- application of theoretical ideas to the work you are undertaking with your clients
- discussion of ethical issues and any ethical dilemmas arising
- discussion of personal material arising from client work which may be impactful for you in terms of content (e.g. you have experienced something similar) or process (e.g. you may manage and respond to things in a similar way, even though the content is different)
- managing responses in the ongoing client relationship
- professional developmental issues.

Many supervision models will argue for a more complex picture with overlaps of the personal and professional, and with ethical and theoretical considerations seen as subsets of these components. Consideration of how you personally would like to work will be included in your selection of a supervisor, which is considered next.

Selecting a supervisor

The selection of a supervisor is usually the primary responsibility of the trainee, unless a placement provider includes this as an integral part of its package. Where the latter is the case, trainees might be fortunate to secure a placement which includes supervisory provision free of charge, whereas for others this service may be subsidised with trainees being expected to contribute a nominal fee. In those instances in which supervision costs apply, this will need to be factored into your assessment of financial circumstances and thus overall readiness to commence placement.

We have already discussed how supervision hours will be undertaken in proportion to practice hours, leading to a specified minimum number of hours completed over the period of an academic year or overall training programme. Besides the hours requirement, training providers may lay down further guidelines to enable you to select a supervisor appropriate to the level and type of training you are undertaking. These guidelines are in turn influenced by professional body requirements. So for example your training provider may specify:

- the type and academic level of qualification your supervisor should have attained
- modality practised by the supervisor
- whether your supervisor should be an accredited/registered member of a specific professional body
- adherence to a specific ethical code or framework
- a minimum amount of post qualification experience as a therapist and supervisor
- that professional liability insurance should be held
- that your supervisor undertakes regular supervision of their supervision practice.

You may also wish to consider your individual requirements and supervisory needs; for example, the times you are available to work with a supervisor, how far you are prepared to travel, and what you would personally value from the supervisory relationship and process. It may be worth revisiting Activity 2.7 for the practical components of this.

It is important, then, that your supervisor is deemed suitable by your training organisation before you commence work with them. We suggest that consideration of these ideas in advance of searching for a supervisor (and indeed in advance of the placement search) makes the formation of a successful working alliance between all parties more likely.

Pre-placement use of supervision

I find it really difficult to see the benefit of being in supervision when I am not actually seeing clients. What is there to discuss if I have not yet started in placement?

Training providers will differ as to whether they require you to have secured your supervision arrangements before starting in placement, but they will certainly require you to be in supervision by the time the first client is seen. The placement you select and gain may offer their own supervision as part of their support to trainees working with them. However, we suggest that some kind of supervisory or consultancy process will benefit you as you start on your placement journey. It can help you to be in dialogue with one or more people about the topics raised in this and previous chapters; for instance, whether you are ready to commence work with clients, your theoretical and ethical understanding, your personal development as well as the practicalities of starting the placement search. As counselling and psychotherapy are relational processes, it makes sense to use professional relationships to explore potential ways in which you might undertake the placement search and application processes together with consideration of the impact these experiences may have on you.

I am struggling financially, and it would be impossible for me to meet the expense of a supervisor before I start in placement. I am looking for a placement where supervision is provided for me for this reason. How can I still undertake this collaborative process of reflection before I start the search?

Some trainees may be in the position where they are unable to afford supervisory support before placement commences. There are other ways in which this dialogue can be undertaken. There may be time allocated to discuss some of these ideas on your training course. Equally, you might decide to get together with one or more of your peers in a professional development group or pairing. In this case, it is important that there is a source (such as your trainer, a more experienced therapist) to which you can refer should questions and/or ethical dilemmas arise.

Contracts

You may be familiar already with some kinds of contracts in your day-to-day life; for example, contracts of employment or those involved as part of the process of renting or buying a home. Also, in the training context you may have undertaken a contracting or group agreement process in which you outlined the ground rules for relating within the training context.

Contracting can be defined as 'an agreement between two or more parties for the doing or not doing of something specified' (see Dictionary.com). The therapeutic contract entered into with your client, therefore, defines the practical and therapeutic boundaries of the relationship as agreed between two parties: the therapist and client (three or more parties if couples or group therapy is undertaken, although in law each client is seen as an individual). Contracting whilst in training and starting in placement can be somewhat more complex, given the number of parties and interests represented.

We have so far discussed the requirements of the training provider with regard to various clinical and academic aspects of the course you are undertaking. All of these

Before You Start: Training Provider and Wider Professional Considerations 75

components are brought together in the contracts agreed by all parties in the placement process: yourself, your training provider, your supervisor and the placement provider.

Sometimes the contractual obligations of all parties involved are amalgamated into one or two contracts, which your training provider may provide, for example:

- A 'three-handed' contract between:
  - trainee
  - training organisation
  - supervisor.

This contract would be used if you started a supervisory relationship before commencing placement. Once starting in placement it would then be replaced by:

- A 'four-handed' contract between:
  - trainee
  - training organisation
  - supervisor
  - placement provider.

Three- and four-handed contracts – The 'hands' in these contracts refer to the needs and expectations of the different parties in the arrangement, and in particular the needs and obligations of the trainee in the context of training, placement and supervision.

Table 3.4 lists some of the common factors contained in these types of contracts, most of which have been discussed in the chapter so far. It should be noted that this may vary according to the training provider concerned.

It is a good idea to familiarise yourself with the contractual expectations we have discussed before you commence the placement search. Preparing yourself in this sense means that when you encounter a potential placement or supervisor you will be able to assess their capacity to meet the requirements of the training course and therefore the contract they will be required to enter and adhere to. This means that any problematic areas can be openly discussed with the parties involved (most importantly with your training provider) to determine suitability, or alternatively whether any adjustment to the contract might be appropriate. You will notice that the three- and four-handed contract does not take into account the client. Your eventual placement may well have a specific contract for work with clients which you will be required to use. If they do not, you can work with your supervisor and the placement provider to construct one appropriate to the context. As mentioned previously, you may need to provide information (or an additional contract) in order to gain informed consent for recording and use of material in academic work.

Further professional considerations

Psychotherapy and counselling are professional endeavours that necessitate a number of steps to be taken before embarking upon practice, albeit likely in an unpaid

TABLE 3.4 Three- and four-handed contracts

1. Trainee therapist agrees to:	2. Training provider agrees to:	3. Supervisor agrees to:	4. Placement provider agrees to:
• work within policies, processes and ethical codes/frameworks as outlined by training provider, which may include: 　○ undertaking client work in a way which enables completion of clinical hours 　○ undertaking supervision in a way which enhances practice, the ability to complete academic work, and within requirements of relevant professional bodies. (May include review of audio recordings of client work) 　○ undertaking supervision within agreed ratios of client work to supervision hours 　○ not to exceed the limits of their competence as a trainee • adhere to agency policies and procedures.	• provide a standard of training which supports competent ethical grounded client work • provide supervisors and placement providers with sufficient information in regard to training and professional registration requirements (where applicable) in order that they are able to meet their contractual obligations • work within specified ethical codes/frameworks • inform the placement provider/supervisor about any serious concerns about the trainee's competence to practise.	• familiarise themselves with and provide supervision in line with training provider and placement provider requirements, which may include: 　○ working within a specified ethical code/framework, and within agreed ratios of client hours to supervision hours 　○ supporting trainee to enhance practice and academic work through review of audio recordings of client work 　○ provision of information (e.g. in a report) in relation to trainee's strengths and areas for development 　○ commitment to inform the training provider/placement of any concerns in relation to student's practice (e.g. serious ethical concerns, frequent non-attendance of supervision) • adhere to agency policies and procedures.	• familiarise themselves and provide placement provision in line with training provider requirements. which may include: 　○ provision of a safe environment in which to work 　○ inducting the trainee regarding policies and processes of the agency 　○ facilitating the trainee to record practice for purposes of professional development and completion of academic work 　○ provision of a named person managing or overseeing the work of the trainee in the agency 　○ pre-assessment and appropriate allocation of clients 　○ provision of information (e.g. in a report) related to work within the agency, strengths and areas for development 　○ commitment to inform the training provider/supervisor of any concerns in relation to student's practice (e.g. serious ethical concerns).

capacity. These considerations, as far as possible, ensure the safety of both you and your future clients whether psychologically, emotionally and/or physically. In this section we discuss duty of care, health and safety, issues of confidentiality and data protection and their practical implications in the professional capacity.

Duty of care

Kent (2012) suggests that therapists have a duty of care to their clients. However, Jenkins (2007) argues that this is not strictly true in the narrow sense of the legal term, suggesting that the duties of the therapist can be more accurately described as ethical or professional; for example, the avoidance of harm to the client.

> Legal dictionary.com describes **duty of care** as 'a requirement that a person act toward others and the public with watchfulness, attention, caution and prudence that a reasonable person in the circumstances would.' Failure to do this constitutes negligence and may result in a lawsuit claiming damages (Hill and Hill, n.d.).

The ethical codes and frameworks set out by professional bodies explain our responsibilities to the client and our intention to uphold these in the service of the client when we become a member. Within the placement context the therapist shares responsibility with the organisation to provide a service that is 'fit for purpose'. The placement agency (or organisation it sits within) should have context-specific policies; for instance, in regard to safeguarding children and vulnerable adults.

Safety for the client and the therapist

You can see from the discussion of duty of care that the safety of the client is paramount. The safety of the therapist is also a key consideration and needs to be factored into any pre-placement preparation. What follows then is a discussion of different aspects of safety, and some practical steps that can be taken to ensure that, as far as possible, the therapist is honouring their ethical and professional responsibilities.

Psychological and emotional safety

Counselling and psychotherapy are activities in which psychological and emotional processes may impact both the client and the therapist. In some approaches, active exploration of emotions is encouraged and is seen as the root of therapeutic change. In others, negative thought processes and responses may be explored and challenged to facilitate change in behaviour. In most placement settings trainee therapists will likely work with clients experiencing varying levels of distress.

The training context is probably the primary setting in which you will learn to work with client distress in a manner appropriate to the model practised. Alongside this, both supervision and personal therapy support the trainee to manage the impact of clients' distress on their own psychological and emotional processes whilst working in placement.

Additionally, the BACP ethical framework and UKCP code of ethics (or other codes where appropriate) include guidelines that facilitate you to consider your own and clients' psychological and emotional safety. For the protection of the client in this respect, training organisations and/or placement organisations may require trainees to become student members of a professional body such as the BACP or UKCP. In this way they can be assured that the trainee is informed and abiding by the relevant code or framework, and is fully aware of their professional responsibilities. Professional membership of these organisations incurs a fee, which is usually the financial responsibility of the trainee.

Physical safety

Traditional talking therapies are not an inherently physical activity, although some therapists (particularly those working with drama, body therapy and similar disciplines) may incorporate movement and body work. This, however, does not mean that the physical safety of both you and your client should not be considered before starting to practise. Your own physical safety may be one of the factors training organisations take into account when deciding whether a placement is suitable, and may form part of the contracts we have previously discussed. Working conditions may be assessed in order to establish whether the placement is a safe enough working environment for you and service users. Public and/or employers' liability insurance may be checked if it is held.

You may also wish to make this a consideration on first and subsequent visits to a placement you are considering working with. This will be discussed in the next chapter, which addresses the placement search in some detail.

Financial safety

As part of your practical considerations, it is important, before commencing practice, to consider how you might cover costs arising from any claim made against you for malpractice or negligence. This type of claim, including associated or legal costs, is mitigated for by professional indemnity insurance. It is usually the responsibility of the trainee to arrange this type of insurance, although occasionally cover is organised by the placement organisation. Additionally, since client work is likely to be imminent the financial viability of continuation in training, and thus provision of a stable relationship for any long-term clients, may be something you wish to consider as part of your ethical considerations about readiness to commence in placement.

Public liability insurance protects members of the public (including clients) who visit premises, against personal injury or damage to their property. **Professional indemnity insurance** is usually the responsibility of the therapist and covers for claims where a mistake has been made or negligence has occurred. (BusinessDictionary.com)

Confidentiality and data protection

We are sure that confidentiality of client material will be included in your induction into placement (discussed in Chapter 5) and has no doubt been covered in your training course. We have also discussed in this chapter how you might ensure that you have informed consent to record and use any client work in written material you produce as part of gaining your qualification and/or professional accreditation/registration. It is worth making the distinction here between 'breach of confidentiality' and 'limits of confidentiality'. In the former, an aspect of client material is disclosed without their consent. You can see that in the case of written work, confidentiality is not breached since the contracting process will ensure the client has given informed consent (see earlier explanation) for material to be used in this way. This, of course does not absolve the therapist from the responsibility of sufficiently anonymising the material in order that the client cannot be recognised.

Other instances of the limits of confidentiality include the use of supervision, safeguarding issues and issues of law such as the prevention of terrorism and money laundering. It is also vital to consider how you will protect the confidentiality of your client in your notes. For example, what material does the placement provider require you to record in case notes? How are notes stored in your placement agency? Who has access to this storage facility? Note keeping is covered in more detail in Chapter 5.

Chapter summary and ongoing reflections

This chapter has covered important pre-placement considerations, building on the theoretical, ethical and personal developmental reflections in Chapter 2. We have covered the requirements of your training provider, including recording and writing about practice, accruing supervised client hours, selection of a supervisor and how you might utilise this support before you start in placement. We have also covered wider professional responsibilities and practical steps that can be taken to ensure these are met.

Learning objectives

Each trainee will have specific expectations of the placement experience in terms of their own personal learning. Setting learning objectives can be useful in that they articulate what you wish to gain and highlight specific steps to enable this.

Learning objectives might include:

- links to training course content about theory and/or ethics
- pursuit of an area of personal and professional interest
- the desire to work in a particular context.

> Learning objectives are specific statements of desired achievement in learning. In the therapeutic context this learning might be professional, personal or a combination of both of these. Objectives may also include some indication of how the goal will be achieved.

Setting learning objectives before you start the placement search can ensure that your search is focused only on organisations that are likely to meet these learning needs. Objectives can be revisited once you are familiar with the placement context, and periodically once in placement to facilitate further planning to ensure continuous professional development.

These reflections based on Kolb's (1984) cycle will support you in considering and setting learning objectives following your engagement with Chapters 2 and 3:

1. Record your thoughts and feelings as you come to the end of Chapters 2 and 3.
2. List one or two main areas of learning.
3. Set any specific learning objectives you consider necessary to be able to commence the placement search. These might be specific learning activities such as reading about confidentiality and data protection, or activities such as enquiring about student membership of a professional body.
4. Set a deadline for yourself to complete any actions you have highlighted in point 3 above.

The following vignette gives an example of one trainee's learning objectives.

Whilst in the first year of training, I was adamant that I would be unable to work with men. However, having had a number of positive experiences working with male peers in my training group I decided to challenge this assumption. In discussion with my trainer and supervisor, I realised that family experiences had given me a particular perception of my own power in relation to men. I feel I am ready to challenge this. Whilst my first thoughts were to apply to a women's centre to ensure that no men would be referred to me, I realise that with appropriate support I can work through this. I am therefore setting myself an objective to look into placements that offer generalised counselling services regardless of gender, and to explore the possibilities further with my supervisor.

Further reading

Hawkins and Shohet's *Supervision in the Helping Professions* (2006) is an accessible introduction to supervision. If you were interested in the type of strategy used in Activity 3.2, you may find the website www.getselfhelp.co.uk useful as there are a number of free downloadable activity sheets for use personally and with clients. For those interested in learning more about mindfulness and meditation techniques, you might access *Meditation for Beginners* by Jack Kornfield (2005), which comes with a useful CD of meditations. Note keeping is covered more in Chapter 5, but you may find Tim Bond and Barbara Mitchels' (2015) *Confidentiality and Record Keeping in*

Counselling and Psychotherapy a useful reference text for ongoing training and when staring in placement. Since regulations in counselling and psychotherapy are constantly being reviewed and updated to ensure rigour and applicability, we suggest checking with the professional bodies that you are, or aspire to be, a member of to ensure that the information included in this chapter is still current.

References

Bond, T. and Mitchels, B. (2015) *Confidentiality and Record Keeping in Counselling and Psychotherapy*, 2nd edn. London: Sage.
British Association for Counselling and Psychotherapy (BACP) (2012) *Accreditation of Training Courses including the Core Curriculum*. Available at: www.bacp.co.uk/admin/structure/files/pdf/11914_atc_scheme09_v2012.pdf (accessed 23.03.14).
British Association for Counselling and Psychotherapy (BACP) (2013) *Ethical Framework for Good Practice in Counselling and Psychotherapy*. Available at: www.bacp.co.uk/admin/structure/files/pdf/9479_ethical%20framework%20jan2013.pdf (accessed 23.03.14).
Despenser, S. (2011) *BACP Information Sheet S2: What is Supervision?* Lutterworth: BACP.
Ellis, A. (1994) *Reason and Emotion in Psychotherapy*, rev edn. Secaucus, NJ: Birch Lane Press.
Feltham, C. and Dryden, W. (1993) *Dictionary of Counselling*. London: Whurr.
Hawkins, P. and Shohet, R. (2006) *Supervision in the Helping Professions*. Maidenhead: McGraw Hill.
Hill, G.N. and Hill, K.T. (n.d.) *Duty of Care*. Available at: http://legal-dictionary.com/_/dict.aspx?word=Duty+of+care (accessed 19.08.14).
Jenkins, P. (2007) *Counselling, Psychotherapy and the Law*. London: Sage.
Kent, R. (2012) *What do Counsellors and Psychotherapists Mean by 'Professional Boundaries'?* Lutterworth: BACP.
Kolb, D.A. (1984) *Experiential Learning: Experience as the Source of Learning and Development*. Englewood Cliffs, NJ: Prentice Hall.
Kornfield, J. (2005) *Meditation for Beginners*, including CD. London: Bantam.
McLeod, J. (2010) *Case Study Research in Counselling and Psychotherapy*. London: Sage.
United Kingdom Council for Psychotherapy (UKCP) (2009) *Ethical Principles and Code of Conduct*. Available at: www.psychotherapy.org.uk/code_of_ethics.html (accessed 06.09.11).

Four

The Placement Search, Application and Interview Process

This chapter will:

- Provide practical support for the work required at all steps of the placement search, application and interview process.
- Enable brief exploration of the circumstances in which placement provision might be set up within an organisation not previously offering this service, and allow reflection on the practical, ethical and professional implications of such an undertaking.
- Offer opportunities for reflection in regard to feedback obtained from potential placement providers in support of continuing professional development.

There is no denying that searching for and securing an appropriate counselling and psychotherapy placement can be a challenging process. The growth in popularity of counselling and psychotherapy as a career choice means there has been an increase in the number of training courses available and consequently a greater number of trainees seeking placement opportunities to further their development. To meet this demand we have seen growth in the number and types of organisations developing counselling and psychotherapy services. Having said this, availability will be dependent upon a variety of factors, some of which we considered within Chapter 1. In some geographical locations trainees may find they are competing with numerous applicants for a limited number of placements. It makes sense then to suggest that thorough preparation will ensure that you are in an adequate position to undertake your placement search methodically, and that this in turn will facilitate your engagement with the application and interview processes.

You have already started this process of preparation in the previous two chapters by considering your personal and professional readiness together with the requirements of your training provider and professional bodies in regard to the placement endeavour. This chapter guides you logically through the next steps by detailing the significant aspects of the search, application and interview processes. We take a look at possible ways in which your individual requirements together with those of your training organisation and the potential placement provider will influence both how and when you submit an application. We consider how your personal qualities and professional capabilities can be best highlighted throughout this process, ensuring that your placement search is as productive and rewarding as it can possibly be. This chapter also addresses the importance of informed choice making in regard to placement offers, detailing the possible steps involved when deciding whether to accept when an offer is received. Equally, there is much to be gained from reflecting on those times when you are unsuccessful in securing a placement offer. For instance, reflection on your experience of the application and recruitment processes and any feedback provided by the placement provider will no doubt support you in preparation for submitting further applications and attending interviews that follow. Finally, we take the opportunity to consider the potential circumstances in which a trainee may be invited to be part of the process of setting up an individual placement or larger therapy service in a setting where one has not previously existed.

What am I looking for in a placement?

As you have undertaken the activities in the previous two chapters, you may have been gaining more of a sense of where and with whom you might like to work. This will enable you to start with some groundwork, which is likely to give clarity and a sense of direction to the process. We acknowledge that the search may not be an easy undertaking and that you might encounter dead ends and/or curve balls along the way. However, it is our hope that having some knowledge about what you are looking for and where to look may give you a positive head start. In Chapter 2 you also started to consider some of the implications of undertaking the placement search. In addition to your personal and professional readiness, this included considering your current life situation and how this might impact upon the placement search in terms of:

- the time available to undertake a placement
- the practicalities of travel
- financial constraints
- accessibility needs
- the type of client group you are considering.

Now would be a good time to return to your responses to Activity 2.7 in which you considered a typical week and your commitments therein. We suggest drawing on this to support your completion of the placement search and application preparation sheet we have provided in Table 4.1. We suggest returning to this planner as you read through the specific sections of this chapter, as compiling relevant information in one place will provide you with an easily accessible framework to aid the search, application and interview processes you will be undertaking.

TABLE 4.1 *Placement search and application preparation sheet*

Personal requirements	Training provider requirements	Placement provider requirements

What is my training provider looking for in a placement?

In Chapter 3 we gave you an opportunity to consider the requirements of your training organisation in terms of the placement provider, for example:

- the possible requirement for a placement in a specific modality/theoretical orientation
- the potential need to audio-record and/or write about and utilise client material for academic purposes
- number of client hours needed to be accrued and period of time allocated for you to undertake this (this might include a possible specification from your training provider that the placement is able to offer a specific number of clients over a week, or other period of time)
- requirements for supervision in terms of hours, level and type of qualification of supervisor, and professional accreditation.

We invited you to reflect on these details in Chapter 3 and to seek advice on any issues you were unclear about through referring to your training course handbook or asking your trainers. We hope that you have sufficient clarity regarding the above or any other specifications made by your training institution. This information should enable you to complete the 'training provider' section of Table 4.1.

Now you have completed these sections, what you have effectively created are the parameters of your search. Once the boundaries are clear in terms of your personal and training provider requirements, you can commence gathering information from potential placement providers and start to find the best fit.

Although not all of the information you need might be immediately available through an advertisement for trainee therapists, or even a service's website, you should now be able to ask relevant questions in order to ascertain if a placement is the right one for you. It is worth considering at this stage how flexible you are able to be with your requirements. If a potential placement means travelling for 10 minutes more each way, is this something you are willing to think about or is this absolutely out of the question?

There may be some requirements which are essential for the placement to meet under the Equality Act 2010. You may have a long-term medical condition or disability, meaning that adjustments will enable you to access an advertised role and indeed the application process. In this case you might want to let the placement provider know this at the point of first contact.

> Under the Equality Act disclosure may not necessarily be compulsory unless an individual is seeking adjustments. For more information, Action on Hearing Loss have a number of fact sheets on rights under the Equality and Human Rights Acts that are widely applicable. They are available from: www.action-onhearingloss.org.uk/supporting-you/factsheets-and-leaflets/your-rights.aspx.

Now that you have a clearer idea what it is you are looking for, a number of options present themselves in regard to how and where you search. Of course you, your training provider and/or supervisor are likely to be knowledgeable in your local area, and there is no way in which we could cover every avenue available to you in this respect. However, there are a number of ways in which you may discover that a placement exists and whether there are opportunities available.

Word of mouth: peers and colleagues

The seeking of placements is a regular and ongoing event within every counselling and psychotherapy training institution. Far from happening at set times or purely at the beginning or end of an academic year, it will be taking place on a rolling basis dependent on, for example, individual readiness and the potential need to seek new and different placements. This means there are a wealth of people who have both undertaken and are undertaking the search for a placement at any given moment. Your institution may well have pre-established communication channels and ways in which the training and graduate community are encouraged to network. For example, there may be an online forum in which you might post the particulars of your requirements for others to respond to. Or you might attend a social gathering where others who are searching for, or who have successfully gained positions, are also in attendance. We have deliberately placed this source first, as fellow trainees and graduates are often a forgotten source of much potential knowledge and information which is ready and waiting to be utilised. In our experience, colleagues are usually more than willing to support each other in this way, and this might mean even informing each other without enquiry as to what opportunities might be available.

Increasingly, we have found that counselling and psychotherapy trainees travel some distance to their training provider. In this case this information local to the provider will be less relevant, and some of the following sections may be of use. In particular you might find networking in local group events where therapists will be in attendance supportive in your search (see later section on networking).

Your training organisation

Each training organisation differs in how and when they communicate with trainees. It is likely, however, that they will receive information from local organisations who are seeking trainee therapists for placement. It is worth familiarising yourself with how this information will be communicated to you. If you know that opportunities will be advertised in the electronic newsletter, for example, then do make sure that you read this when it is sent to you (we know how easy it is for these things to get lost in the depths of an inbox or even in our spam folders). Find out where posters advertising placements will be displayed and make time to visit. Your trainers may also be a source of information for placement opportunities.

Placement or job fairs

Placement fairs may be run by your training provider, a placement provider or other agencies wishing to showcase what is available and to recruit local candidates. Equally, you may find jobs fairs advertised, at which you might make useful contacts able to inform you about organisational counselling services, such as those within universities or local authorities.

Electronic media

Individuals differ in terms of their familiarity with and confidence in using electronic sources. The placement search is one time when having access to a computer with an internet connection can be an invaluable tool. If you do not own a computer, you should be able to access one through your training organisation, local library or internet café.

Searching on the internet is a different kind of active search, which means setting out search parameters additional to those that you defined in Table 4.1.

It is out of the scope of this section to be able to provide a detailed set of instructions on how to maximise the use of a search engine, so the following is a brief overview to help get you started.

In order to search the internet you will need to decide which search words you are going to use. It is useful here to be as specific as possible, as this will ensure that your search returns results as relevant as possible to your requirements. Nevertheless, be prepared that you will need to search through a large amount of information before you find what you are looking for. To give an example, typing

> Depending on the specifics of your training, the search terms you use may be changed slightly. For example, 'counselling psychologist', 'psychological wellbeing therapist' or 'psychological wellbeing practitioner'.

the words 'counselling' and 'Nottingham' into Google today returns 1,290,000 results.

Of course, some of the web pages are going to be much less relevant than others, and you might find that relevance starts to wane after about page four or five of the listings. For example, 'counselling Nottingham women' returns 877,000 results and 'counselling Nottingham women ethnic minorities' 857,000. This might suggest that your search will be narrowed the more specific you are about the type of client group you wish to work with. The search 'hits', however, will be reflective of the number of agencies working in the area – the more specialised the field, the fewer agencies there are likely to be offering services.

Other online sources are available in addition to generalised search engines. Websites such as www.counselling-directory.org.uk/ have the facility to search by location and postcode. There is the facility to narrow down searches to organisations only (since search results will also include all independent therapists practising in the area); www.jobsincharities.co.uk/ lists voluntary roles in the sector, which may sometimes include counselling roles. Sites such as www.jobs.ac.uk/ list opportunities in the educational sector. Keep in mind that some of your 'hits' may not be agencies at all but private therapists working with particular client groups, so careful filtering is needed even if you have been specific with your search parameters.

We suggest that further support may best be gained from peers, your training provider, IT department or student support services where appropriate, or through further independent research into the area.

Newspapers

You may find that the best place to search for placements in your local area is in the local press. The main bulk of job advertisements are normally included on the same day every week, so you may wish to make a point of buying the paper on that day and make a note of the main section in which volunteer posts appear. National newspapers also advertise volunteer roles. For example, the *Guardian* has a social supplement which has a section for jobs in health and social care. You can also access the online versions of the jobs pages of newspapers. For instance, by going to http://jobs.guardian.co.uk/jobs you can selects the types of jobs you are interested in from drop down lists, or type in key words such as 'counselling' to see what is currently available.

Professional bodies and organisations and related periodicals

Two of the main professional bodies for counselling and psychotherapy in the United Kingdom are the British Association for Counselling and Psychotherapy (BACP) and the United Kingdom Council for Psychotherapy (UKCP). The websites of these organisations (www.bacp.co.uk and www.psychotherapy.org.uk) may offer information about opportunities. More specifically, if you are a member of these organisations you will receive their periodicals – *Therapy Today* and *The Psychotherapist* – in which both paid and volunteer roles are advertised. If you are not yet a member you may find that your training organisation receives these periodicals and encourages you to access them (e.g. in the library or learning resource centre).

Networking at events: conferences and continuing professional development

As a trainee therapist you will no doubt attend events and courses supplementary to your core training that contribute to your continuing professional development. At these events you will meet fellow professionals both in training and qualified who can potentially assist you in your search for placement opportunities. There are a couple of ways in which this might happen:

- through active networking and discussion with other delegates
- through enquiry at the organisational stands which often appear at these events (conferences in particular).

This is a time when being clear about your motivations, potential client group and practical needs will be particularly important. For example, you might find yourself in discussion over lunch with the manager of a placement organisation or their associates. Speaking with authority and clarity about yourself and your approach will leave a lasting impression, meaning an invitation to apply is more likely to be forthcoming. At the very least those with whom you network are likely to know others who might be in a position to support your search. We would encourage you to be active in either obtaining or sharing relevant contact details. You might consider having some business cards printed for this purpose.

Making initial contact

During the course of your search there will be some information that is easily available from the publicly accessible details you find. However, some information may not be immediately apparent; for example, whether the placement agency is currently recruiting, or whether you are permitted to audio-record work with clients. In these cases it may be necessary to contact organisations to find out more. This contact might typically be by phone or email. If you are contacting by phone, it is useful to have a list of questions to ask in advance to avoid the need of calling again with questions you have forgotten. Getting the name of the person(s) in charge of placement recruitment is always useful so that this person can be contacted directly. It is a good idea to save emails to draft and return to them later to check for typographical errors, that you have struck the tone and level of formality you were aiming at, and that all the information you need has been included.

> If you do decide to have some business cards printed, this can be done quickly and cheaply via a number of popular internet sites. Remember that you should seek advice from your trainers as to how you might describe yourself professionally. Although, at the time of writing, the terms 'counsellor' and 'psychotherapist' are not protected in the United Kingdom, this does not mean that it is appropriate to describe yourself as a counsellor or psychotherapist until you are fully qualified. We suggest it is important to consider what is appropriate and ethical in this regard. Finally, ensure that you include telephone and email contact details.

Recording the results of your search

Each trainee will have their own way of recording the results of their search according to individual preferences. The means by which you record your findings is less important than actually making a note of them somewhere, such as:

- a simple notebook
- your training journal
- a spreadsheet created for the purpose
- index cards.

We have provided a sample record sheet as Table 4.2 for you to copy and use as a pro forma.

Deciding where to apply

Once you have gathered information about potential placements you will need to make decisions about which of these organisations you wish to apply to. Of course, it is entirely up to you whether you apply to one or more organisations. Some trainees decide to deal with one application at a time, taking learning from the success or otherwise of each to

TABLE 4.2 *Placement search record form*

Name of organisation	Contact details	Main contact name	How are training provider and personal requirements met?	Additional notes (if applicable)

inform later applications. Others decide to apply to more than one placement at a time. What is important here is that you have a clear rationale for either approach. If you are applying to more than one placement, you need to ensure that you have some way of managing the simultaneous application and interview processes that will ensue.

Activity 4.1 invites you to consider the pros and cons of each placement you have gathered information about to support you in the process of deciding where to apply.

Activity 4.1 Evaluating placements and deciding where to apply

Aim

- To enable consideration of the pros and cons of each placement you have researched in order to support decision making about applications.

Background

The activity of searching and applying for a placement may necessitate gathering of information about a number of organisations. Evaluating the particulars of the organisation against your own practical and developmental needs will contribute towards finding the right placement for you.

Activity

Whilst reviewing the information you have gathered for each potential placement, consider the following questions:

- How well does this placement meet my practical needs?
- How well does this placement meet requirements as set out by my training provider?
- If I were to apply for this placement, what would be the potential in terms of:
    - accumulation of supervised client hours
    - personal development
    - development of philosophical and theoretical understanding
    - development of ethical understanding
    - development of wider professional skills and competencies.
- Which of my own skills and qualities would contribute to the effective delivery of this placement (with clients and otherwise)?
- How do I see my potential for development as a practitioner within this placement?

A PDF version of this activity is available to download from https://study.sagepub.com/oldaleandcooke

---

You may wish to record these ideas in the 'additional notes' section by each placement in Table 4.2. If you have used another means of recording your placement search, record the results of this activity in your own way.

Once you have completed this activity for each of the placements you are considering, one or more may stand out as being preferable. If this is not the case, you may seek further advice from peers, tutors or your supervisor (if you have one) to consolidate the options you have and to support your decision-making process. Some of the information in Activity 4.1 may not be available until you attend interview and we would therefore suggest that you make a note of any outstanding questions so that these can be addressed should you secure an interview.

Applying for a placement

Once you have identified which placement(s) you wish to apply for the application process can commence. The level of detail given by placement providers to potential applicants may differ from organisation to organisation. Some may have a formal advertisement with a full person specification and job description. Some may simply issue a statement; for example, by email to let trainees know that they are recruiting.

> A **job description** will give potential applicants the details of the available role. It should outline the duties expected of the potential post-holder, and sometimes includes further details of who they will report to, as well as additional details about the organisation. A **person specification** outlines the qualifications and personal attributes an applicant should possess.

If a specification is available, you can evaluate this information to ensure that you meet the criteria set by the agency, as far as possible, and that you are willing to undertake the role as stated. However, do not be put off if there are some gaps in your skills set. Most person specifications set out both 'essential' and 'desirable' qualities. If you do not currently possess one of these, or you see it as an area for development, it is possible to show how you plan to work towards this. Of course, if there are numerous gaps you may wish to discuss the application with a supportive other to deem if it is appropriate to apply for this particular placement opportunity. If a person specification and job description are not available, you may wish to contact the placement provider to clarify what they are looking for. Some placements ask solely for an application form, others may be willing to receive a curriculum vitae (CV) in addition to this. The compilation of these is discussed in the next sections. It is worth noting the placement providers' preferred method of returning the application: some will request a paper-based submission, others may accept email applications, in some instances the provider may make use of online systems of application.

Application forms

It is not possible for us to cover the structure and format of every possible application form here. However, there will be some commonalities between all forms. Most will ask for:

- **Personal details** – name, address, contact details.
- **Education and qualification details** – grades and educational levels, including any qualifications pending or being currently worked towards.

- **Work experience** – including the most recent paid/voluntary roles undertaken and sometimes details of duties involved.
- **A personal statement** – outlining the skills and qualities you possess that will enable you to successfully undertake the role within the organisation.
- **Demographic details** – such as gender, ethnic origin and whether you consider yourself to have a disability will sometimes be gathered confidentially for the purpose of compiling equal opportunity statistics.

Filling in all details as accurately as possible is important. It may be a good idea (if you have not already) to gather together relevant information and documentation such as qualification certificates or transcripts or letters of confirmation which outline the stage of your current training and your academic achievement; if your training provider issues a letter or certificate confirming your suitability or readiness to commence placement, it will be vital to include this. This will support you in completing and submitting application forms and will also ensure that you have them to hand if copies are requested at interview or at the point of an offer being made.

Writing a personal statement

The personal statement section of the application form is where you have the opportunity to sell yourself to the potential placement provider. This might include:

- illustrating why this particular placement opportunity appeals to you (this could include mention of your knowledge of the organisation and what it offers)
- outlining the qualities and skills you possess that make you particularly suitable for the position
- examples of your strengths and reference to areas for development and how you are working on these – placement providers are interested to see your reflexivity.

Several years ago we decided to alter our placement recruitment processes so that the process more closely matched the standard job application and interview format of the jobs market, thinking this would be useful experience for trainees who will eventually be seeking employment in the field. Experience has shown that many applicants seem to struggle with the personal statement aspect of the application, often including irrelevant information or missing opportunities to demonstrate why they want the placement and how they are suitable for the position and our organisation. We are also looking for enthusiastic applicants who can show evidence of wider skills, such as an ability to write clearly and persuasively, so clarity of thought and a clear structure are equally important as content in the statement.

As this example illustrates, placement providers will have a set of criteria by which they assess your application and the personal statement you submit. Knowing what the placement is looking for is consequently a key component in ensuring that your personal statement is relevant. This is where revisiting the role profile, person specification and/or the placement advertisement is important. Knowing your own competencies and qualities and matching these to the role is also essential. Striking a balance between demonstrating that you meet the specified criteria and that you have an awareness of your areas for development will ensure that you illustrate this self-knowledge and that you have some understanding of the requirements set out by the organisation (and the wider profession). It is important to highlight the steps you are taking in regard to any areas in which you fall short of the requirements. Also, using concrete examples of what you have achieved is one way in which you can show your areas of competence. At this point it is useful to revisit Chapter 2 activities to draw together useful information to include in your personal statement (this will also be useful when reflecting on possible interview questions). Activity 4.2 enables you to draft a personal statement for use on either a specific or multiple applications as appropriate.

Activity 4.2 Preparing a personal statement

Aim

- To enable compilation of a personal statement with concrete examples of skills and competencies.

Background

The placement application will include a section towards the end of the form called 'additional information' or 'personal statement'. After completing the sections related to personal details, education and employment, this empty box is your opportunity to 'sell' yourself – to impress the potential placement provider. The application form will usually include instructions outlining how to complete this section; for instance, 'please use the space below to describe how your skills, knowledge and experience relate to the requirements of the role and for any other information you consider relevant to your application for this placement' or 'please use this section to explain why you feel you are suited to this placement and what you can bring to it with reference to the person specification'. Knowing what the placement organisation is looking for, your own skills and qualities and matching these to the role is essential. Use this section to show that you are motivated to undertake the placement and that you have carefully considered why you believe you would be successful. A good personal statement strikes a balance between strengths and areas for development and includes explicit examples to illustrate points.

Activity

Use Table 4.3 to help you compile your personal statement. We have indicated some areas you might wish to include; however, it will be vital to amend these in line with any person specification to ensure that you tailor the statement to the specifics of the placement being applied for. Remember to note specific examples of when strengths have been demonstrated.

TABLE 4.3 Preparing a personal statement

Person specification headings	Strength	Development	Specific example(s)
Knowledge and application of theory			
Understanding and application of ethics			
Therapeutic skills and attitudes			
Personal resilience/personal development			
Additional areas specific to job description/person specification			

A PDF version of this activity is available to download from https://study.sagepub.com/oldaleandcooke

We also offer the following tips in the hope that this further supports you to compile personal statements that contribute towards successfully obtaining a placement:

- keep your statement short and tailored to the specifics of the placement being applied for
- read your statement out loud to ensure that it flows succinctly
- show it to a trusted friend, colleague or your supervisor (if you have one) for a second opinion
- remember to review your statement in regard to each application – you should tailor it to emphasise those areas most closely matched to the particular placement opportunity.

Organising your curriculum vitae (CV)

Some placement providers may require you to submit a CV with your application. Indeed, you may decide to send a CV with a covering letter to organisations you are interested in; this is a proactive way to make yourself known even if no opportunities are currently available. CVs are sometimes kept on file and potential applicants contacted when a vacancy becomes available.

Having worked in my family's business since I left University, I had no idea where to start when asked to submit a CV by a potential placement provider! What did they want to know? How should the CV be structured? I felt uncomfortable about admitting I didn't know what to do but took the risk to speak to one of my trainers, who reassured me that although I was daunted there were lots of resources online to support me to successfully complete the task. I found numerous useful tips about content and even found free templates to download which provided a structure for my CV.

A number of CV templates are available online or in word processing packages such as Microsoft Word. CVs usually have standard sections which may include:

- name, address, contact details
- date of birth
- a brief personal statement
- educational history, highlighting achievements and how these are quantified
- employment history
- further information such as:
    - voluntary roles undertaken
    - other courses and training undertaken which might complement your role
    - hobbies and interests.

The CV you construct for a therapeutic role will differ from the one you use for other job applications and we recommend adapting your CV to ensure that information specifically relevant to the profession of counselling and psychotherapy is given more prominence. As mentioned earlier, when considering the construction of a personal statement keep in mind that your CV will require review so that it can be tailored to the specifics of each placement opportunity. An example is included as Figure 4.1 to give you an idea of the structure and kind of information included. We hope that this is useful for you to adapt for your own purposes.

Curriculum Vitae

Zee Greenwood
Date of Birth: 30.01.1968
3 The Woods, Alson, RX32 7LT
Contact: 07927 888823
zee.greenwood@anymail.com

I am a second-year counselling trainee on the Diploma in Integrative Counselling at Alston College.

Qualifications
Diploma in Integrative Counselling – Alston College (due for completion June 2015)
NVQ child care – Alston College (2000)
5 GCE O'Levels A-C including Maths and English – Alston High School (1986)

Work Experience
2000 – Present (full-time to August 2012, currently part-time) Child Care Assistant – Alston Day Nursery, Chancery Road, RX42 9TR
1998 – 2000 Retrained in child care
1986 – 1998 Full-time self-employed – ZG Car valet, Alston, RX4 8NW

Volunteer Roles
1999 – 2004 Childline – volunteer counsellor

Courses and professional development
June 2014 – Working Creatively in Therapy (1 Day, Alston Therapeutic Associates)
December 2014 – Working with Trauma (2 Days, Alston College)

Hobbies and Interests
As part of my self-care I enjoy cycling for fitness. I raise money through charity bike rides, the most recent of which was London to Brighton. I enjoy arts and crafts, in particular crochet.

FIGURE 4.1 *Example curriculum vitae – placements*

What follows are some additional tips to support you in compiling a relevant CV:

- keep your CV to no more than two pages
- reverse chronology is the preferred format
- create a strong personal profile or opening statement which is informative (e.g. how you meet the requirements of the placement provider in terms of level of training or qualities desirable)

- most placement providers seem to prefer a conventional format that is easily accessible, so avoid photos, coloured paper, fancy fonts
- be clear, accurate and appropriate – check for grammatical, spelling and typographical errors
- avoid repetition between CV content and your personal statement.

Referees

All placements will ask for one or more referees. Some organisations may provide a pro forma for this purpose whilst others may ask for a letter or email from a referee outlining key aspects of your competence as a trainee therapist. It may be that you must cite a trainer as one of your referees. Even if this is not compulsory, your trainer should know you well enough to be able to vouch for your professional readiness (whether or not a formal assessment has been undertaken).

Sending off your application

Once your application is complete, ensure that you send it to the placement agency via the route they have requested to minimise the likelihood of delay in processing. Some organisations may receive applications by post, some electronically via email and/or online application systems. Some may allow application via any of these means. Make sure you have included all of the supporting information needed (e.g. your CV, evidence of your 'readiness' to commence placement, copies of relevant qualifications or academic transcripts).

Speculative applications

It may be that you are applying to a number of organisations speculatively, or to one particular organisation that you have an interest in working with, even if they are not advertising. In this case it is even more important to adjust your CV and covering letter to match the organisation and their requirements. This shows an attention to detail which makes it more likely that your information will be held on file even if no vacancies are available at the time of writing.

Interviews

You have spent a fair amount of time considering and identifying which particular placements are of interest to you and what information you should include in an application in order to present yourself in the best light as a trainee therapist. Now comes the time when the placement will consider your application and decide whether they are able to see a fit between you and their organisation. If they do determine potential in your application it is likely you will be invited for an interview, which may take one of a number of formats. These interview formats are explained below along with some suggestions about how to prepare for each. However, it should be kept in mind that applications for placements sometimes exceed the number of positions available and indeed even the organisation's capacity to interview. Try not to be too discouraged if you do not get invited to interview and remember this is the first opportunity you have to ask for feedback to improve future applications. Therefore, if the communication from the agency does not specify why you have not been offered an interview, do ask for feedback regarding your application and what might have made it more successful.

The individual interview

The individual interview will take place either one-to-one between you and an interviewer, or may involve a panel of interviewers representing different aspects of the placement organisation or therapeutic team. Occasionally the panel might consist of stakeholders such as governors or trustees, who may not be directly employed by the organisation but have an interest in its aims and mission. It some instances, a service user representative may also be included on the interview panel.

Types of group interview

There are two basic types of group interviews: a candidate group and a panel group.

In a candidate group interview, you will most likely be put in a room with other placement applicants. In some cases, these applicants will be applying for the same position as you, in others there may be more than one placement position available. During a candidate group interview, you can expect to be asked to listen to information about the company and the placement opportunity and you may be asked to answer questions or participate in group exercises. The group-based interview may be an observation of your interactions with a group of people during induction or training, or a pre-defined activity.

In a panel group interview, you will most likely be interviewed individually by a panel of two or more people. This type of group interview is almost always a question and answer session, but you might also be asked to participate in some type of exercise or test that simulates your potential work environment.

The group interview is designed to enable the placement provider to get a sense of how you work with others, and whether this will be supportive of the organisation and counselling services therein. The placement provider will be looking for applicants who can contribute well to a group discussion without dominating it. They may be looking to see whether you demonstrate independent thinking as well as an ability to interact with others to achieve a group task or goal. This may sound simple but can be a challenging experience, as the following trainee's account demonstrates.

During the interview I was expected to take part in a group task with others who had applied for the same placement opportunity as me. Although I had thought about this possibility I found it very difficult to participate in the group and said very little, albeit that I had lots of ideas about how to go about the task and what the interviewers might be looking for. I came away from the interview deflated and disappointed in myself. I decided to discuss my experience in personal therapy and also with members of my training group. I identified this was a theme and decided to work on being more active in discussions within my training. This really helped in other interview situations and I found myself more able to assert my views in a group context.

With this in mind, it may be worth reflecting on your experiences of interacting in the group setting in training to identify your strengths and areas for development as part of your preparation for the group interview context. Finally, here are a few tips to consider in regard to the possibility of a group-based interview:

- To prepare:
    - practise active listening and communication when in a group context
    - use your research about the specific placement/organisation to anticipate possible group-based scenarios
    - develop your knowledge of ethics and your ability to apply this in practice.
- In the group interview:
    - clarify your understanding of what is required by the interviewers
    - be actively involved, listening and speaking effectively
    - try to involve others
    - keep track of time
    - ensure that you contribute to the group, remaining focused on the activity as set.

The practice-based interview

During some interviews you may be asked to undertake a therapy session with a person acting in the role of client. This will be designed to evaluate your counselling skills and attitudes, and whether your approach matches that which is needed by the organisation. Sometimes sessions may include an ethical dilemma for you to work with. Alternatively your understanding of ethics may be evaluated by another means, such as an interview question. If you are called upon to undertake an interview of this type you may wish to revisit the material in Chapter 3 which supports preparation for the readiness assessment.

Presentations

Occasionally a placement provider may ask an applicant to present their knowledge of an aspect of professional practice. In some instances you will be informed of the topic and equipment available to you in advance; however, there may be times when you are not made aware of this until you arrive for the interview itself.

I wasn't too surprised when I arrived for my placement interview and was asked to put together a short presentation – my trainer had suggested this would be a possibility and had recommended some ways to prepare for this in advance. I drafted a possible presentation structure before the interview and took this with me to refer to as a prompt. This really helped as I was anxious as soon as the word 'presentation' was mentioned! Another tip that worked in my favour was my trainer's recommendation that I also take along a brief description of how to work through an ethical dilemma. The presentation topic included a short overview of a scenario I might encounter in practice and I was asked to show how I would address this! The interviewers said they were impressed that I had relevant materials with me and was openly willing to use these. I was so pleased to hear that this contributed to me being offered a placement with the organisation. One thing I learnt from this is that interviewers do not expect you to keep all knowledge in your head and that they are also looking for a wider set of qualities and skills than those I had been learning about in my observed skills sessions within training.

Whether informed in advance or required to construct a presentation as part of the interview process, we recommend choosing presentation media you are comfortable using; this might include visual aids, such as neatly written flip-chart pages or bullet points on a PowerPoint slide. You may feel more at ease simply using the spoken word. Again, preparation will be the key to success. We suggest the following format to support you when compiling a presentation:

- tailor the presentation to your audience wherever possible; consider what they will know and what you will need to explain, and what are the key points you wish to put across
- plan your presentation. Ensure that it has a clear structure, for example:
  - a brief personal introduction
  - an explanation of your intended structure with indication that you will respond to questions at the end of the presentation
- the aims of your presentation
- any background to the issue and the content of your points; for instance, what you are saying and why this matters
- conclusions – a short summary of the key points you have made
- any questions.

You may find it useful to rehearse your presentation so that your interview is not the first time you run through the content. Also, it can be beneficial to ask a friend or colleague to watch your presentation so that you can get some feedback in regard to content and possible tips relating to the manner in which you present the material. Undertaking a dummy run will assist you in ensuring that you keep to time boundaries and enable you to identify and make necessary alterations in preparation for the interview process. On the day, make certain you have all your presentation materials with you (e.g. a memory stick if using an electronic presentation package, any notes, handouts or visual aids). It can be useful to consider in advance how you might cope if something goes wrong; for example, emailing a copy of your presentation to yourself as a contingency against memory stick problems or having paper copies of your presentation notes to refer to if equipment malfunctions. Remember to speak clearly at a steady pace; try to engage your audience by making eye contact with each of them as you speak. Finally, it is important to note that it is your strengths as a developing professional being assessed rather than your ability to pull together a technologically advanced, all-singing, all-dancing presentation.

What is the placement provider looking for?

Broadly speaking, the placement provider is likely to be looking for understanding of all of the areas we have discussed in previous chapters. Hence interview questions or activities might well include assessment of:

- understanding of theory (training and/or placement specific)
- therapeutic skills and attitudes
- ethical understanding
- personal readiness and development
- knowledge of the organisation and your 'fit' within it.

The final bullet above points to the fact that the placement provider is extremely likely to want to know that you have awareness (and/or a willingness to learn about) and knowledge of the particular clinical and ethical demands of the specific client group and organisation. In this respect, researching the organisation in advance is essential so that you can incorporate this into your responses, or ask questions about pertinent points if appropriate.

As mentioned earlier within this chapter, placement providers are also likely to be looking at your wider skills base, and this may include your:

- ability to work in a team and to communicate effectively with people inside and outside an organisation
- written skills and IT proficiency
- capacity to make decisions and creatively solve problems
- ability to plan, organise and prioritise work
- ability to obtain and process information
- long-term potential.

Now might be a good time to revisit the activities you have undertaken in Chapters 2 and 3 in order to compile a list of your strengths and areas for development which might provide useful points for discussion in interview. Remember that the interviewer(s) will not be trying to catch you out, but will want to know that you can engage thoughtfully

The Placement Search, Application and Interview Process

with these areas of professional importance in order to establish your suitability to undertake a placement in their organisation.

Possible questions and responses

Given the types of interview above, and the areas of your practice which are likely to be assessed in interview, it would be useful to undertake Activity 4.3 which invites you to think about the possible interview questions or scenarios that you are likely to encounter. It may be useful to undertake this activity taking into account each placement for which you are invited for interview. In this way the particular considerations of each organisation and client group can be fully considered.

Activity 4.3 Possible interview questions

Aim

To enable you to anticipate possible interview questions, scenarios and responses.

Background

Interviews may be:

- structured and based on specific elements of therapeutic work; for instance, 'Give me an example of how you have empathised effectively with another person'
- semi-structured, so you might be asked a follow up question; for example, 'How did you know this was effective and what did this tell you about the impact of empathising with others?'
- unstructured, although this tends to be less commonly used, as this format does not support interviewers to draw comparisons between applicants.

Regardless of the format used, there are some predictable areas you can prepare for.

Activity

1. Consider the questions in Table 4.4 and provide responses with examples from your developing practice. You may wish to draw on responses to other activities to support you to complete this.
2. List further questions and suggested responses informed by your research on the organisation, the placement job description and/or person specification.

(Continued)

(Continued)

TABLE 4.4   Possible interview questions

Question	Possible response with examples where appropriate
We've read your CV but can you tell us about yourself?	
What are your strengths and areas for development as a trainee counsellor/therapist?	
What can you contribute in particular to this organisation?	
Give an example of how you dealt with an ethical dilemma.	
What is your theoretical orientation and how does this inform your practice with clients?	
What other placements have you applied for? Why? Which would be your preferred placement?	
Why do you think we should offer you this placement opportunity?	
Explain your interest in this agency/this client group.	
How do you imagine being impacted by this client group and/or presenting issue and how do you think you would manage this impact?	
Do you have personal experience of the specific issues clients accessing this service are likely to explore and, if so, how might this impact your work with clients and your own self-care?	
What questions do you have for us?	
Insert possible questions based on the person specification	

A PDF version of this activity is available to download from https://study.sagepub.com/oldaleandcooke

Interviews may be:

- structured and based on specific elements of therapeutic work; for instance, 'Give me an example of how you have empathised effectively with another person'
- semi-structured, so you might be asked a follow up question; for example, 'How did you know this was effective and what did this tell you about the impact of empathising with others?'
- unstructured; although this tends to be less common as this format does not support interviewers to draw comparisons between applicants.

Regardless of the format used, there are some predictable areas you can prepare for. For instance:

- 'We've read your CV, but can you tell us about yourself?' (this is often used as an opening question)
- 'What do you think are your strengths as a trainee counsellor? What are your areas for development?'
- 'What other placements have you applied for? Why? Which would be your preferred placement?'
- 'Why do you think we should offer you this placement opportunity?'
- Based on issues related to the placement context/client group, you may be asked questions such as 'How do you imagine being impacted by XYZ and how do you think you would manage this impact?' or 'Do you have personal experience of XYZ and, if so, how might this impact your work with clients and your own self-care?'
- 'What questions do you have for us?'.

In preparing for placement interviews, it can also be useful to practise responding to possible interview questions as the following trainee illustrates.

In my supervision group I shared my fears about interview failure and was relieved to hear that I was not alone in feeling this way. Our supervisor suggested we work together as a group to prepare for interviews, so we decided to meet as a peer group to interview one another. We adapted the skills observation process used in our training so that we had a structure – interviewer, interviewee and observers – and took turns being interviewed. I found the feedback helped me to improve my performance in the subsequent peer group meetings. When it came to attending actual interviews, I felt prepared and I'm certain this helped reduce my anxiety and improve my performance. I would recommend getting together with peers to practise in this way.

Presenting yourself in the best light and avoiding self-sabotage

Whilst we might all work towards an interview with the best of intentions, there are probably few of us who can honestly say that there is not an internal critic or saboteur, who makes life hard for us at times. It is worth remembering that the physiological signs of anxiety (e.g. increased heart rate, sweating and faster breathing) are actually designed to help us cope in difficult situations as part of the 'fight or flight' response.

> The 'fight or flight' response is a physiological reaction to a stressor in the environment. In evolutionary terms, our primitive ancestors would have benefited from responses such as increased heart rate, dilated pupils and surge of adrenaline as it would have enabled them to either flee a threat or aid the hunt for food. The response persists today, though it is unfortunately triggered in response to more benign situations as well as those where we are presented with actual threat.

The release of adrenaline that ensues can actually enhance our performance by focusing our energy. However, too much can be debilitating, so finding ways in which to manage anxiety responses is vital. Knowing yourself and the kinds of processes which can both support and sabotage you in the process of application and interview can be invaluable in controlling anxiety and preventing us finding a stick to beat ourselves with rather than presenting ourselves in the best possible light. This 'stick' usually has some basis in a message we have internalised during interactions with others. Depending on which therapeutic model you work with you may give it a different name. Cognitive behaviourists might call it 'negative self-talk'. If we are person-centred we might talk about 'conditions of worth'. Transactional analysts might see it as a 'critical parent'. What is common here is that this aspect of our experience can work for us or against us. We need to work out whether there is any aspect of the process that has a basis in reality and use this to our advantage. For the sake of using a single metaphor we will use the cognitive behavioural notion of 'errors in thinking' here (see Branch and Wilson, 2010). These can take a number of forms, and for each Table 4.5 gives an example linked to how it might impact you during an interview.

Luckily, there are a number of practical strategies cited to support you to overcome the impact of potential 'erroneous thinking'. We have listed some of these strategies along with alternative kinds of 'self-talk' which may help to keep you focused in an interview situation. If by the time you come to the end of this section you feel that your struggles and fears will not be addressed by the strategies Branch and Wilson (2010) propose, we suggest speaking to your trainer, supervisor or any supportive other to devise a way of working this through to best prepare you for the interview situation.

Some practical top tips – on the day of the interview

We have covered a lot of ground in this chapter about the pre-preparation you can undertake to make success in interview more likely. However, what about on the day itself? It's worth running through some common-sense practical tips, which we are sure you already have in mind:

- Get enough sleep the night before the interview.
- Try to fit in some kind of relaxing activity beforehand. This will vary from person to person. Yoga and meditation might work for you. Equally it might be reading, walking or playing on the games console!
- Leave yourself time to eat and drink beforehand (there is nothing worse than having a rumbling tummy or a really dry mouth when you are trying to make a good impression).

TABLE 4.5 Errors in thinking (adapted from Branch and Wilson, 2010)

Thought error	Definition	Example	Coping strategy	Alternative
Catastrophising	Imagining disastrous results arising from an event which is minor.	'Oh no, I didn't shake the hand of the interviewer. That's it I'm never going to get it now!'	• Putting thoughts into perspective. • Focus on Coping.	'Okay we are just at the start of the interview, I can still make a good impression and shake their hand on the way out.'
All-or-nothing thinking	Thinking in extremes, or black-and-white thinking.	'I always perform badly in interviews, so why bother!'	• Be realistic. • Develop less extreme (both/or) reasoning skills.	'I know I have a tendency to do X in interviews, I'll practise with a friend.' 'Even if this interview didn't go well I can learn from it for the next.'
Fortune-telling	Predicting the outcome of events before they are clear or decided.	'I'm bound not to get the role, I won't bother going.'	• Test predictions. • Take risks. • Understand that the future is not entirely shaped by past.	'Okay, I'm going to risk going to the interview; worst case scenario I can learn from the feedback.'
Mind-reading	Imagining you know what another person is thinking.	'What does that smile mean? They are laughing at me, aren't they?'	• Think of alternative reasons. • Accept you may be wrong. • Ask, if appropriate.	'Ah, maybe I reminded them of a private joke, I might be mistaken …' Smile back …? And if appropriate, ask.
Emotional reasoning	Taking feelings as facts.	'I'm so nervous so I will botch this up.'	• Balance thoughts and feelings. • Give time and space.	'I've done lots of preparation and so think I will be okay. I'll take some time to read through my notes, or go for a walk to calm down.'
Mental filtering	Only acknowledging information that backs up your beliefs.	'That was a really rubbish response to that question.'	• Become aware of the positives. • Accept compliments!	'The interviewers seemed to be engaged with what I was saying, and I think I performed well overall.'

- Make sure you know where you are going, who you are going to see and at what time.
- Check if you need any identification or any other documentation and make sure you have this with you. For example, some placements may ask for identification to be provided for a Disclosure and Barring Service check before a formal offer can be made.
- Read through your copy of the application and any notes you have made, including questions for the interviewer(s). Take a copy with you if possible, so you can refer to it to check that you have not missed anything you wanted to get across.
- Know how you are going to get to your destination and leave extra time in case of delays/difficulties in parking and so on. (On the other hand, arriving too early and having to wait can be equally anxiety provoking, so having a good idea of how long travel will take will also save some anxiety.)
- If you are driving, finding out where to park beforehand and having the necessary change if needed can be a real help.

> The Disclosure and Barring Service (DBS) runs checks to help 'employers make safer recruitment decisions and prevent unsuitable people from working with vulnerable groups, including children.' This service replaced the Criminal Records Bureau (CRB) check in 2012. Your chosen placement agency will let you know if you need to undertake a DBS check to work with them and what the process is. (For more information, see Disclosure and Barring Service, 2012.)

- Additionally, remember that the interviewer(s) want you to perform well and will not be trying to catch you out. Try to relax, enjoy and learn from the process.
- During the interview:
    - try to make eye contact to engage the interviewer(s)
    - present yourself positively and honestly
    - try to maintain open body language
    - listen to each question and check back with the interviewer(s) if you are not clear what is being asked
    - show you have researched the organisation and the placement opportunity in advance
    - demonstrate your enthusiasm and desire to learn and develop.

After the interview – reflexive practice

So, you have come through the interview and you are now waiting to hear the outcome. Will you get the placement position or not? At this stage it is best to avoid 'post-mortems' or going over and over the interview in your head. There is nothing that you can do to change the outcome now whether you feel you performed well or not. Watch out for and address any fortune-telling behaviours we highlighted in Table 4.5 to ensure that you are not escalating or exacerbating anxiety whilst waiting for the outcome of your interview.

When you do hear from the agency that you have either been successful or otherwise, it is well worth gaining feedback on the interview. In either instance the feedback can support you in any future interviews you will undertake. Agencies will differ in how they offer feedback and the level of detail. Some may offer informal feedback over the phone; others may offer written feedback by letter or email. Do not be afraid to ask specific questions if this is relevant. When you have the feedback you need, it can provide a starting point for developing specific action points to further your development and interview technique. For example, some agencies may pinpoint opportunities to improve responses to specific interview questions, which will allow you to develop these in readiness for the next opportunity that arises. Activity 4.4 provides a basis to evaluate feedback and develop strategies and points of development for future interviews.

Setting up your own placement

It is beyond the scope of this book to go into the practice of setting up your own placement in any great detail. However, if you are in the position that this becomes a possibility it will be important to reflect upon a number of questions with the support of your supervisor and training provider to decide if this is the right course of action for you. Additionally, there will be a number of procedural considerations to take into account before the placement and service you are offering 'goes live':

- Am I in a position to be able to offer a service which:
  - is realistic, given my current situation and practical circumstances?
  - can be started up and sustained within the organisation as it currently exists; for instance, is there the funding and resources to make this work?
  - is in line with the organisation's overall mission and aims, and if not what will the implications be for the counselling service and overall organisation?
  - meets the needs of my training provider in terms of their requirements of a placement organisation?

Equally, there are questions to be asked that will impact on feasibility:

- How many clients can realistically be seen and how will they be managed in terms of referral, assessment, ending?
- Who will write policies, procedures, contracts and ensure that these are in line with the agency's wider policies?
- Is there private space available for a sufficient length of time to set up a service of this nature?
- Who will manage start up and ongoing running of the service? If not you, are there the resources available to do this?

As you can see, all of the above questions and more need to be carefully considered before embarking on this endeavour; it is by no means impossible, but we reiterate the importance of carefully considering all of the questions in conjunction with your trainer and supervisor before taking this step.

Activity 4.4 Reflecting on feedback

Aim

- To facilitate consideration in regard to placement provider feedback in order to develop an action plan in support of future applications and interviews.

(Continued)

(Continued)

Background

Whether or not you are successful in securing a particular placement, it can be useful to ask for specific feedback about how you did within the recruitment processes. We suggest making a note of all feedback received so that you can use the information gained to develop your future performance.

Activity

Use Table 4.6 to summarise specific areas of feedback, reflect on your responses to these comments and devise appropriate action points for development in the area. We have included an example to support you in this endeavour.

TABLE 4.6 *Reflecting on feedback grid*

Feedback point	Comments	Specific points for development
(Example) Need to provide more detailed ethical knowledge and show how I would relate this to client work.	On reflection, I think I applied too early in my training – we hadn't completed the ethics module and so my knowledge was limited and I wasn't prepared. Although I've now passed this component, I still think my understanding needs work.	1. Become more familiar with ethical frameworks/codes of professional bodies. 2. Practise applying knowledge to ethical dilemmas taken from the literature. 3. Use supervision and/or peer support to explore the above.

A PDF version of this activity is available to download from https://study.sagepub.com/oldaleandcooke

Chapter summary and ongoing reflections

This chapter has considered the placement search, application and interview processes, as well as continuous reflexivity and development whether or not you are initially successful in your endeavours. We have stressed the importance of preparation and hope that you now have the means to compile a bank of useful material to support the ongoing search. The following areas of reflection may further support your future planning:

1. Record your thoughts and feelings as you come to the end of Chapter 4.
2. List one or two main areas of learning, whether this be striking or useful new information or realisation of gaps in your knowledge or resources.
3. Set any specific learning objectives you consider necessary to develop your learning or fill any gaps identified. This might include activities as diverse as compiling or updating a CV, or gaining the technological knowledge needed to be able to undertake an online placement search.
4. Set a deadline for yourself to undertake any actions you have highlighted in point 3 above.
5. Use the support of others in the preparation process as much as possible!

We wish you all the best, whether you are in either the early or ongoing stages of this process.

Further reading

There are a number of books available which support CV writing and the application and interview process. Though not specific to counselling and psychotherapy, Corinne Mills' text *You're Hired! How to Write a Brilliant CV* (2009) goes into detail about structure, content and format. Judi James (2009) authors a text on interview techniques within the same 'You're Hired!' series. James Innes has written two 'definitive guides' to CVs and covering letters: *The CV Book: Your Definitive Guide to Writing the Perfect CV* (2012) and *The Cover Letter Book: Your Definitive Guide to Writing the Perfect Cover Letter* (2012).

References

Branch, R. and Wilson, R. (2010) *Cognitive Behavioural Therapy for Dummies*. Chichester: Wiley.
Disclosure and Barring Service (2012) *Disclosure and Barring Service*. Available at: www.gov.uk/government/organisations/disclosure-and-barring-service (accessed 21.08.14).

HM Government (2010) *The Equality Act*. London: Stationery Office.
Innes, J. (2012) *The CV Book: Your Definitive Guide to Writing the Perfect CV.* Harlow: Pearson Education Ltd.
Innes, J. (2012) *The Cover Letter Book: Your Definitive Guide to Writing the Perfect Cover Letter.* Harlow: Pearson Education Ltd.
James, J. (2009) *You're Hired! Tips and Techniques for a Brilliant Interview*. Richmond: Trotman.
Mills, C. (2009) *You're Hired! How to Write a Brilliant CV*. Richmond: Trotman.

Five
Commencing Placement: Managing Practicalities, Processes and Relationships

This chapter will:

- Support you in the process of settling into your new placement by inviting you to consider significant aspects of your placement context including agency policies and procedures (such as conventions for assessment, referral, contracting and note keeping).
- Consider how the requirements of your training provider may be successfully incorporated into your work; this will include reference to academic work where applicable and examine how your client caseload can be appropriately built up.
- Examine how the network of relationships involved within placement provision may be utilised to best effect.
- Discuss reflexivity and use of supervision both in support of early placement practice and in the development of professional identity as experience is gained and competence increased.

This chapter is based on the assumption that you have been successful in gaining a position as a trainee therapist within a placement organisation. If so it will be immediately relevant to you and may be usefully accessed at various points throughout your time with an agency as part of your continuing reflexive process. If you are not yet in the position of having secured your placement provision and are reading ahead, the information contained within this chapter could usefully support you in searching and applying for a placement. Knowledge about the processes involved in working with clients and other stakeholders in the placement organisation may also be relevant to interview preparation.

Our intention within this chapter is to support you to begin the process of beginning and settling into your placement by highlighting how an induction process might be undertaken. We explore aspects of the agency that are important for you to know about from the outset, including both therapeutic and wider service issues. We look specifically at the different ways in which clients might be assessed and referred to you. In addition, consideration is given to the experience of meeting your first client. Significant aspects of agency and training provider requirements are discussed in regard to contracting with clients. We address issues concerning how you might appropriately build your client caseload, utilising supervision to support you in this endeavour. The wider network of relationships is examined together with how these might be used to best advantage in your early placement practice.

During this chapter we specifically refer to audio recording and writing about aspects of your work with clients and/or wider placement experience. By discussing these important components of your practice, we hope that you are able to consider how the various aspects of the placement process might be managed to ensure that you are able to complete the academic and/or professional component required by your training provider. Writing about practice takes many forms and some of these were discussed in Chapter 3 when we initially considered the requirements of your training provider. At this point, you may find it useful to have to hand your training course information relating to the pieces of work you need to complete and notes made in regard to activities completed when reading earlier chapters. As mentioned previously, this will enable you to access relevant information when completing forthcoming activities and considering the points we make through subsequent sections of this chapter. No doubt, at some point in your early placement experience you, your training provider and supervisor will be concerned with how things are going. The theme of assessing practice in placement starts in this chapter with a look at how all parties will make an assessment of how you are progressing. In Chapter 6 these ideas will be developed, and decisions about continuing or ending a relationship with a placement provider are specifically addressed.

Inevitably we will be unable to cover every eventuality of your particular placement within this chapter. As highlighted in Chapter 1, placements are diverse enterprises with many factors influencing their operation. Additionally, readers may be working with a variety of ethical codes/frameworks as well as agency specific policies and procedures, resulting in often complex and highly individualised requirements. However, we hope to have highlighted general themes about starting in placement which will be useful for most trainees. With this in mind, Activity 5.1 invites you to actively consider what you need or want to know about your placement agency at this early stage in your relationship with them. In this way we hope you are prompted to find answers to any questions you might have and that this, in turn, provides a firm foundation on which to start building your placement experience.

Activity 5.1 Familiarising yourself with the placement organisation

Aim

- To support you to become familiar with your placement organisation.

Background

It may well be that the placement you secure has a formal induction process designed to familiarise you with different aspects of the running of the organisation, the therapeutic services within it, and practicalities including the layout of the building and important policy and procedural issues.

Activity

Using the questions below, consider what would be *essential* to know and *useful* to know about your placement organisation. You might consider aspects such as:

- the organisation itself; for example, in regard to both therapeutic and wider functions of the organisation
- the building you will be working in
- client group
- work with clients
- policies and procedures:
    - about the counselling service
    - about other aspects of the organisation such as accessibility policies, health and safety.

Consider how you might gather the information you have identified and from whom.

A PDF version of this activity is available to download from https://study.sagepub.com/oldaleandcooke

As the main receptionist and office manager for a counselling charity, I am responsible for the induction process for new volunteers. It's great when a volunteer comes prepared for the induction process as it ensures nothing is missed, and that each volunteer is on the lookout for information that is particularly relevant for them.

Getting started – planning to begin your placement

The excitement and relief at obtaining my preferred placement was soon replaced by anxiety – I hadn't anticipated the severity of this! I went to speak with my tutors about it and they were great in supporting me to put some of my fears into perspective as well as reminding me to utilise other people – my therapist and supervisor – in my support network! Accessing support really helped me to explore my responses and to find ways to reassure myself that I wasn't expected to know everything before I started. The placement is part of my training, where I will gain so much learning.

I decided to drive to and from my new placement at different times of the day before I started. I really needed to know how long the journey would take because I had to factor the school run into the equation. I felt more confident and prepared knowing this in advance, and ticking this off my long list of actions was a bonus!

Having secured your placement and knowing when it is going to begin means you can now start planning in more detail. As indicated in the examples above, this might include some practical steps as well as finding ways of coping with the psychological and emotional impact of beginning something new. Just as we emphasised the importance of preparation in regard to the search and recruitment processes, we wish to highlight how continuing your preparation will assist in stress reduction and enable you to direct energy into successful placement learning. You are no doubt aware that the ability to *plan* and to put plans into action are essential skills for the therapist to possess. Trevithick (2005: 144) suggests two ways of thinking about planning that we see as applicable to the trainee therapist's preparation: a reflective approach and a checklist approach.

We have adapted these approaches into Activity 5.2, as we see value in each as well as the complementary nature of adopting the two.

Activity 5.2 Beginning placement – approaches to planning

Aim

- To support you to continue your preparation for commencing placement by exploring both reflective and checklist planning.

Background

Just as we emphasised the importance of preparation in regard to the search and recruitment processes, we wish to highlight how continuing your preparation will assist in stress reduction and enable you to direct energy into successful placement learning. You are no doubt aware that the ability to 'plan and act' is an essential skill for the therapist to possess. Trevithick (2005: 144) suggests two ways of thinking about planning that we think may be applicable to the trainee therapist's preparation:

- A reflective approach.
- A checklist approach.

Activity

1. *Reflective planning* – the following questions are designed to support you to reflect on:

    o your thoughts and feelings related to beginning your placement
    o how best to manage these.

   Use Table 5.1 to record your reflections.

TABLE 5.1 *Beginning placement – approaches to planning 1*

How do I feel about the prospect of beginning this placement?
What am I most anxious or concerned about?
Why am I anxious or concerned? How can I address these responses?
How have I managed similar anxieties in the past?
What am I looking forward to in this new endeavour?
What am I confident about?
What can I do to make the most of these responses in support of beginning my placement?

2. *Checklist planning* – Table 5.2 includes some suggestions (adapted from earlier chapters) to think about when beginning your placement. You may wish to adapt or add to this list to ensure that your individual circumstances are addressed.

(Continued)

(Continued)

TABLE 5.2 *Beginning placement – approaches to planning 2*

Checklist planning		
Have I planned for:	**Completed Y/N**	**Any action?**
Family commitments		
Work/life balance		
Self-care		
Travel time to and from placement		
Time for personal therapy		
Time for supervision		
Finances		
Keeping in touch with peers		
Study time/assignment deadlines		
Additional areas I need to consider:		

A PDF version of this activity is available to download from https://study.sagepub.com/oldaleandcooke

Beginning and settling into your placement – the induction process

When we refer to the dictionary.com definition of the word 'induct' we can see that it has a number of connotations. These include notions of:

- installation into a particular place
- an introduction to something new which needs specific knowledge or experience
- to be drafted in as a member to (e.g.) a new profession.

So, as you work through the sections on settling into your placement, the first two of the above will be explicitly addressed. We will then think about how you may:

- familiarise yourself with the organisation and building in which you will be undertaking your new placement
- undertake processes related to client work which are specific to your placement organisation, such as referral, contracting, assessment and review and note-taking procedures.

All of this is, of course, part of your early professional experience and, as such, all of the discussions in the chapter are relevant to the third point of the definition above. Professional considerations for your future career as a counsellor or psychotherapist, such as professional registration or accreditation and continuing professional development will be addressed in Chapter 6.

It may well be that the placement you secure has a formal induction process designed to familiarise you with different aspects of the running of the organisation, the therapeutic services within it, and practicalities including the layout of the building and important policy and procedural issues. Induction may be undertaken in one or more ways:

- as part of the interview/recruitment process
- before or alongside commencement of the actual placement
- formal or informal induction with a 'mentor' or line manager within the agency, which may be one-to-one or a group induction with other volunteers/new staff (both therapists and other staff).

Inductions may last varying amounts of time and are conducted with varying amounts of formality, but many will cover the points listed in Table 5.3. If they do not, you may find these tables, as well as your responses to Activity 5.1, useful as you start to engage with the placement organisation to elicit the important points you will need to know about working within the organisation.

We have divided Table 5.3 into questions of who, where, when, how and what and separated them into two sections concerned with your work with clients, as well as the wider organisation and buildings they are located within. There is some overlap of information between the two sections, but by separating out information in this way we hope to illuminate the different components effectively. The next part of this chapter will look at each of these areas in a little more detail.

TABLE 5.3 *Induction considerations*

	Preparing for work with clients			
	Who	**Where**	**When**	**How**	**What**
Assessment	Who will assess clients?	Where are initial assessments stored and for how long?	When are clients assessed – how long from assessment to referral?	How are clients assessed? Is this compatible with my core model of practice, and do I need to undertake a further assessment based on this to support my written work?	What is the rationale for assessment?
Referral	Who will I receive client referrals from? Who will contact the client to make the initial appointment?	Where is referral documentation stored?	When will I receive my first referral?	How will I receive a referral?	What kind of clients will you refer to me to ensure that I work within the limits of my competence as a trainee?
Contracting	Who makes the initial contract with the client? On the occasion I need to break confidentiality, who within the agency can help me?	Where is the contract stored?	When does the initial contracting take place – at assessment stage or by me in the first session?	How do I contract with the client? Do I need to incorporate anything further or use a separate contract for informed consent to record work with the client and use material in written work?	What is the basis of the contract with the client (boundaries, timing, length of sessions, number of sessions etc.)? What are the limits of confidentiality according to agency policy?
Note keeping	Who will see my notes? Only me? My supervisor? My agency line manager?	Where are notes stored and for how long?	Am I expected to complete notes immediately following the session?	How do I complete my notes? How do I manage any reflective or process notes I write to support me with my assignments?	What should be included/not included in my agency notes?

Preparing for work with clients (continued)

	Who	Where	When	How	What
Review	Who undertakes the review process?	Where will the review paperwork be stored?	When/how often does a review take place?	How do I assess the ongoing effectiveness of the relationship/therapy? How do I decide if it is the right time to work towards an ending? How do I make an onward referral?	What should be included in my review?

Getting to know the organisation and building(s)

	Who	Where	When	How	What
Becoming familiar with the building	Who do I contact for: – maintenance of the building, repairs? – first aid? – health and safety issues?	Where are: – toilets? – staff only areas? – client areas? – fire escapes?	When is the building closed for annual holidays?	How do I gain access to the building/my work area? How do my clients gain access to the building?	What are the building opening hours?
Becoming familiar with the organisation	Who oversees the organisation overall and how does this fit with my role, the role of my line manager?	Where is the organisation based? Are there other locations and if so, what are their functions?	When was the organisation established? Are there any changes planned for the future which will impact on my role?	How was the organisation established/what is the history of the organisation and how does it link to its mission overall and my role?	What is the overall mission of the organisation and how does it impact the counselling service/my work as a therapist?

(Continued)

TABLE 5.3 (Continued)

Getting to know the organisation and building(s) (continued)

	Who	Where	When	How	What
Other staff	Who undertakes what role and which of these people will I be working with? Who do I directly report to and what is their main role? Who else will be in the building when I see clients?	Where is the counselling service located? Where are the other staff I will be working with located? Where do I find important contact details?	When are other staff available (e.g. my line manager, supervisor, receptionist)?	How do I contact other staff within the organisation, both within this building and elsewhere?	What are the functions of any other teams/individuals with whom I will be working?
Health and safety	Who is responsible for: – health and safety – fire safety – safeguarding	Where is the accident book located? Where are the fire exits?	When are the fire alarms tested?	How do I report an accident or emergency? How do I respond if there is an emergency or threat to mine or my client's safety?	What are the processes for evacuation in the event of a fire or other emergency? What is the safeguarding policy? *If applicable:* What is the lone working policy?
Accessibility	To whom should I report an accessibility issue?	Where are accessible entrances, toilets and loop system if available?	When is equipment such as hearing loops tested?	How can I ensure that my counselling practice is accessible in line with agency policy? For example, how are interpreters booked/loop system used?	What is the agency policy regarding accessibility?

Induction into the organisation

Chapter 1 discussed the nature of the placement organisation in terms of:

- the sector in which it operates
- its mission and intended client group
- factors influencing its operation, including available resources and wider socio-economic factors.

These components may well form part of your induction into the organisation, and once you find yourself in the placement context the influence of these factors may become more obvious to you in terms of the day-to-day operations of the organisation. You will find yourself at the heart of a system comprising interaction between a number of complex factors and processes, some of which are highlighted in Table 5.3.

Each organisation will have policies and processes which ensure the safe running of the organisation and the protection of those who work within it. These include, amongst others:

- health and safety
- fire risk and safety
- first aid
- lone working (if this is a possibility).

It is likely that the above requirements will be covered in your induction and that their communication to you is a requirement of your training provider, so do ask if these are not mentioned.

The building

It is likely that your placement organisation will have one or more premises from which they conduct their business. If the organisation has a function other than counselling or psychotherapy, the buildings may contain a number of different sections or departments with a space designated specifically for therapeutic services. There are a number of important factors to know about the building you are working within, some of which will be linked to its day-to-day use; other points will be specific to your work with clients. Some practical things you will need to know are:

- How and when can I gain access to the building?
- How can I make a phone call, send an email or letter or make a photocopy if I need to?
- Where can I store my belongings whilst I am working?
- Where are the toilets, staff rooms, service user areas?
- Where are the rooms in which I will see clients and how can these rooms be booked?
- Where are the fire exits, alarms and extinguishers? The first aid kits and accident book?

Other considerations to take into account are issues of accessibility. So if, for example, a hearing loop system, access without stairs or a wheelchair accessible room are required, how would the organisation accommodate this adjustment to allow access to the building and services?

> The Equality Act (2010) legislates for the responsibilities of individuals and organisations in regard to access for employees and service users.

Some placements may offer therapeutic services in the client's home, or a location other than the premises of the organisation (such as a GPs surgery or client's workplace). If this is the case, there are further aspects of the environment to consider. When there is a specific space for counselling to take place, this can be set up in a way that is as therapeutic as possible, with a minimum of extraneous distraction. This may not be the case if you are working in a client's living room, or borrowing a GP or nurse's consulting room to undertake a session with a client. When working in a client's own home, the lone-working policy of the agency will be applicable and your agency will no doubt wish to carry out a health and safety check and/or risk assessment prior to committing to working within a particular client's home to ensure the appropriateness of the context and your safety.

My initial placement was undertaken with an agency who offered counselling in the client's own GP surgery. This was a relatively new endeavour for the Health Centres concerned. It took some time to educate the staff at the centre (even with a 'Do Not Disturb' sign on the door!) that it wasn't okay to pop into the room mid counselling session to pick up an item they needed. There were other practical things too, such as remembering to bring a travel clock along (as staff sometimes relied on their computer clocks so there was occasionally not one in the room) and asking for an extra chair to avoid being seated on a huge doctor's chair and my client on a tiny plastic chair (or vice versa).

It took a while to get used to working in my client's home when my agency started offering this service. Quite detailed information was sent to clients before our first meeting to let them know we should have a quiet space where we shouldn't be disturbed. This didn't always transpire, or they hadn't read the information, so a reminder was sometimes necessary. Equally, I found that I learned a lot about my client from their surroundings, which I wouldn't have done had they visited the agency premises. I found myself frequently taking this to supervision to discuss.

One thing that I anticipated and explored before commencing work in a client's workplace was the possible impact that being there might have on them, particularly if it was work-related issues they wanted to discuss. Also, I wondered if they might associate me with the company even though I was working with an independent organisation. Because of this, discussion around these issues within our contracting was particularly important.

The people

As you get to know the organisation it will be important to become familiar with the other staff working within it. Are these volunteers or paid staff? What role do they each undertake and who is it most likely you will be liaising with on a regular basis? It is likely that you will be introduced to these colleagues as a matter of course and that it will be made explicit to whom you will report directly, and who will supervise you (assuming this is a service offered to you by the agency). It is probably useful to know how the organisation functions overall in terms of the people within it. There may be an organisational chart you can refer to which indicates lines of responsibility. Of course there are some things that an organisational chart cannot tell you; for example, the culture of the organisation and satisfaction amongst those working there. These are things that you might be told about or learn through experience of working in placement.

Though I was informed in interview that my placement agency was awaiting funding to ensure the following years' services, I could not have anticipated the impact of this on the working atmosphere. A number of people were on edge, including the counselling team. I felt it was important to discuss this in supervision in terms of possible impact on client work, because of my own nervousness, and the potential for imminent endings.

Multi-agency working/other agencies in the field

As mentioned previously, the organisation in which you will be undertaking a placement does not exist in isolation. It is part of the network of services in various sectors which offer help and support of various kinds to service users. It is likely that referrals will be taken from and passed to other organisations and professionals within the field. Equally, it is possible that at some point you will need to liaise with someone from another service with regard to your client and their wellbeing. The likelihood of this will depend on a number of things:

> The charity Mind have produced a really useful guide to navigating the complex field of 'who's who' in mental health settings. Their glossary of health professionals and organisations is available online (see Mind, n.d.).

- the limits of confidentiality as set by agency policy
- gaining explicit consent from your client for the sharing of such information
- whether your client is working with any other professionals in the field (e.g. a support worker or community mental health nurse).

Induction into therapeutic practice

One function of working in placement is to accumulate hours towards your supervised practice total in order to meet the requirements of the training course you are undertaking. The placement serves other developmental and personal functions as we have mentioned in previous chapters, and we will talk later about related activities you might undertake in placement. However, building up hours necessitates working with clients and there are a number of stages of the therapeutic process which you will have learned about in training. These practical stages of the therapeutic relationship are represented in Figure 5.1.

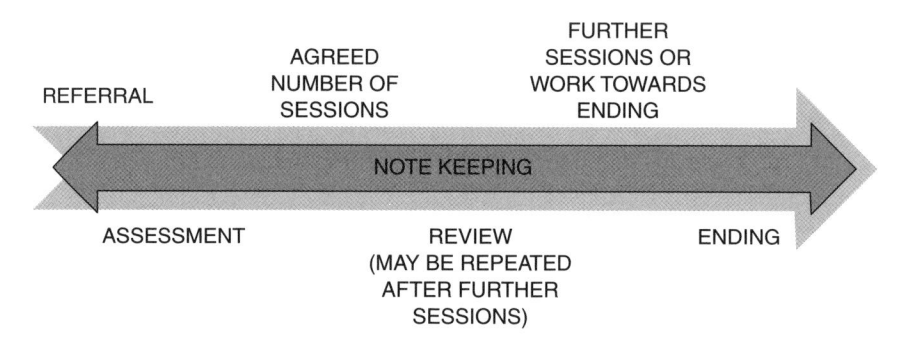

FIGURE 5.1 *The therapeutic process*

Before the relationship between the therapist and client commences a referral is made, either by the client themselves or another party such as a GP. An assessment of the client will be undertaken, perhaps as part of a first session or prior to allocation to a therapist. Equally, contracting may be undertaken at the point of assessment or within the first session. The therapist will make post-session notes throughout the therapeutic relationship and this will support them in, amongst other things, conducting a review with the client as to how they consider therapy is progressing. Dependent on the type of contract offered within the organisation, an ending date might be agreed or if possible further sessions offered to the client. If further sessions are offered, another review or reviews may be undertaken at later points periodically throughout the duration of the contract. As agencies are likely to differ in the ways in which these activities are undertaken, it is beneficial to ensure that you are familiar with the specific requirements of your placement provider. The following sections offer some ideas for further consideration from which you might wish to construct a checklist of information you need to gather prior to the first session with a client.

Referral

In order for an agency or organisation to take on a client they will need to receive a referral.

Referrals may be received from a GP or other source and will depend on the nature and type of the organisation as discussed in Chapter 1. For example, in a secondary educational setting, referrals to a school counsellor may be received from parties such as (but not restricted to) parents and carers, teachers and school support staff, as well as students themselves. What is important in the referral process is that the person being referred is aware of the referral and has a desire to undertake counselling or psychotherapy. Alternatively, a person may refer themselves to a counselling service if they believe it would benefit them and if self-referrals are accepted by the organisation. As part of your process of settling into your placement it is useful to consider the sources from which your placement provider receives referrals and how this might impact the therapeutic relationship and/or process.

> Feltham and Dryden define a referral as a direction 'to counselling or alternative source of treatment' (1993: 157). Therefore, a referral might be made to the agency in which you are working by a party who has deemed therapy to be beneficial to the potential client. Equally, you and/or your client may decide at the outset or during the course of therapy that an alternative service would be more beneficial, in which case an onward referral would be made to another therapist or service (e.g. by you, the client or your agency).

My placement is within the prison service and referrals are received through prison officers, medical and psychological staff. Sometimes counselling is part of an overall offender rehabilitation programme. In my induction with the prison counselling service we discussed how this type of referral might impact on the motivation of clients undertaking counselling and how we might manage this. This allowed me to be transparent with clients about the necessity of their attendance but to work with them to define their own aims and aspirations within this. This felt important in terms of the ethical principle of Autonomy.

I work for an agency supporting young people in full-time education. I find that motivation to engage in counselling varies, but is best when referral has been a collaborative process between teacher (or other support staff) and the client.

As the above examples illustrate, client engagement in the referral process is critical to the establishment of an effective working alliance or for therapy to commence. How referrals are received and the context in which therapy takes place will not only impact motivation, but may also influence other aspects of therapy.

Receiving referrals as a therapist

Once an agency has received a referral (whether assessment is undertaken by you or by, for example, a more experienced therapist), at some point the client details will be passed to you in order that you can start to see the client. Agencies may differ as to how they pass referrals to you, and a lot will depend upon the logistics of the organisation. Some of the possibilities are:

- the client is discussed in a face-to-face meeting with your line manager, mentor or supervisor (if supervision is undertaken within the organisation)
- details are sent securely via email (perhaps using passwords and encryption to ensure security of the information being sent)
- details discussed with the therapist via telephone
- details are kept securely on paper or via an online system which the therapist has access to.

Regardless of the manner in which you receive the referral, once you have the details it is your responsibility to keep these safe and secure and to handle the information in line with relevant agency policy and ethical frameworks/guidelines. Agencies will normally allocate clients a code which is referred to in communications with you, in order to ensure that personal details about the client (e.g. the client's reasons for attending therapy) are kept separate from their name and other personal details. We will discuss legalities of how client data is handled, including the aspects of the data protection act which apply to you as a therapist, in the section on note keeping later in the chapter.

Making best use of referral information

Along with the name of your client, the referral will include other information which will support you in your work with the client. Again this will vary according to the agency, but some common factors may include:

- presenting issue(s) – the reasons the client is coming for therapy
- demographic details
- any diagnosed medical, psychological or psychiatric conditions
- any medication the client is taking
- any risk factors (e.g. suicidal ideation or safeguarding issues).

This information will give important details and background about the client. It is possible that, even with minimal information, we will start to build a picture of the client; for example, their appearance, how they might act, assumptions about gender. These assumptions have the potential to support you in the therapeutic process by pointing to *your* process in relation to the perceived client. Equally, if left unchecked these assumptions may have an adverse influence; for instance, hindering relationship development by limiting empathic understanding and communication. The assumptions may linger and become so ingrained that you are unable to meet the client openly and free of bias – a requirement common to all ethical codes and frameworks. You might like to undertake Activity 5.3, which presents some words/phrases which might commonly appear within a client referral. It is designed to show you how seemingly neutral information can start a chain reaction of assumptions whilst supporting you to think about how you might manage this in your practice. You may wish to revisit this activity, perhaps with the support of your supervisor, when you receive referral details for your first or subsequent clients using some of the actual details you have been given.

Activity 5.3 Assumptions about the client

Aim

- To enable consideration of any assumptions about clients which may arise when you receive referral details.
- To support you to decide how these assumptions may be useful or otherwise to therapy.

Background

Along with the name of your client, the referral will include other information including:

- presenting issue(s) – the reasons the client is coming for therapy
- demographic details
- any diagnosed medical, psychological or psychiatric conditions
- any medication the client is taking
- any risk factors (e.g. suicidal ideation or safeguarding issues).

It is possible that, even with minimal information, we will start to build a picture of the client in our head; for example, their appearance, how they might act, assumptions about gender. These assumptions have the potential to support you in the therapeutic process by pointing to *your* process in relation to the perceived client. Equally, if left unchecked these assumptions may have an adverse influence; for instance, hindering relationship development by limiting empathic understanding and communication. The assumptions may linger and become so ingrained that you are unable to meet the client openly and free of bias – a requirement common to all ethical codes and frameworks.

Activity

Select one of the following words/phrases and write it on a piece of paper:

> Taking anti-depressants
> Professional
> Alcohol problem
> Abused in childhood
> Anger issues
> Low self-esteem
> Religious crisis
> Unemployed

With your selected word/phrase at the centre, note any associations which come up for you in immediate response. Keep going until you feel you have exhausted all your responses. Note even seemingly unrelated associations, as they may be relevant. When you have finished, consider what these responses can tell you about yourself and your process:

(Continued)

> *(Continued)*
>
> - How might reflection in this regard support you with a client referral which contains this word/phrase?
> - How might you support yourself to see the client beyond these assumptions?
>
> You may wish to revisit this activity, perhaps with the support of your supervisor, when you receive referral details for your first (or subsequent) clients, using some of the actual details you have been given.
>
> *A PDF version of this activity is available to download from https://study.sagepub.com/oldaleandcooke*

Onward referral

There may be times when you decide with your client that another therapist, service or a different form of therapeutic input would be beneficial; this may occur at the outset or during the course of therapy. This may necessitate an onward referral to another therapist or service. Of course, this is not always as a result of client factors. There may be times when you receive a referral which you decide, in collaboration with the agency and your supervisor, is beyond the limits of your competence (BACP, 2013: 2). In most cases agencies will endeavour to make referrals to you that are appropriate to both your level of training and personal circumstances; this may be explicitly stated in the contract between your training and placement organisations. Having said this, material may arise, once therapy has commenced, which places a case outside your competence level, for example. In such an event, we recommend familiarising yourself with the placement provider's policy and procedure in regard to onward referral (whether this be made within or outside of the service). The following provide examples encountered by trainees within their placements.

The client's original reasons for attending therapy became overshadowed by the unexpected death of one of his parents. As my agency specialises in short-term work addressing issues related to seeking employment, the counselling coordinator indicated that an onward referral was necessary. I struggled with this decision initially and worried about how to discuss this with the client, as well as how to make a referral should the client agree. With the help of my supervisor I identified a possible referral source and explored ways in which to address this with the client. I need not have worried too much as the client was glad to have the support in finding an alternative service better suited to his immediate needs, and he also had the option to return to our service at a later date.

In the third session with my new client, they started to discuss material which made it clear that we had a number of social connections, including mutual acquaintances which linked our friendship groups. In discussion with my supervisor it was determined that the connections were close enough to necessitate onward referral. This was discussed with the client and a referral made in-house to another counsellor.

My partner was unexpectedly diagnosed with a serious health condition during the final year of my training. The impact of this had far-reaching consequences and with the support of my supervisor and trainer I made the difficult decision to take time out from training and my placement. This meant ending with each of my clients and supporting those who required ongoing counselling to find suitable arrangements. This was a difficult process for me, but I learnt a lot about myself and how to undertake different forms of referral.

Contracting

In Chapter 3 we defined a contract as 'an agreement between two or more parties for the doing or not doing of something specified' (Dictionary.com). We highlighted that a therapeutic contract defines the practical and therapeutic boundaries of the relationship as agreed between two parties, the therapist and client (three or more parties if couples or group therapy is undertaken).

Therefore, in contrast to the three- and four-handed contracts we discussed in Chapter 3, the contract between you and your client will normally contain elements specified by the placement agency including, for instance:

- An outline of the type of help you are offering. This will avoid confusion between other types of support, advice, practical action, friendship or more intimate relationship.
- Number, frequency, timing and length of sessions.
- Fees (amount, how to pay – if applicable).
- The Code of Ethics or Ethical Framework you work to (e.g. BACP, UKCP, BPS).
- Confidentiality and its limits.
- Specifics related to record keeping (how they will be used, who has access and how records are stored).

Contracting tends not to be a one-off activity. It is possible that you will need to revisit or even renegotiate the contract periodically; for instance, when you encounter a situation not explicitly addressed within the initial contracting process or when something occurs that breaches the original agreement.

In my placement in the probation service the limits of confidentiality within the contract are somewhat different from those of my other placement. There are certain rules in place within the hostel in which the therapy takes place that have to be incorporated. For example, there is a 9.30pm curfew and if a client discloses that they or someone else intends to break the curfew, I am bound to disclose this to the officer in charge on that day. This and the other limits to confidentiality are discussed with the client in detail at the start of the therapeutic relationship, and are reiterated regularly.

Later in the chapter we will discuss how you might specifically contract for the other ways in which, as a trainee, you might need to make use of information about your client and the relationship; for example, as part of writing about your practice in an academic piece of work.

Assessment and review

Once a referral has been received by an agency, generally an assessment of the client will be undertaken. The assessment process will depend upon a number of factors, including the setting in which the therapy takes place and the type of therapy offered. In some settings standard systems may be used to assess clients, such as the Clinical Outcomes Routine Evaluation (CORE) (www.coreims.co.uk/). This assessment and review tool enables a client to rate themselves on a number of measures in terms of how they have been feeling over the past seven days. The number of questions asked varies. These tools can be useful in that they enable the therapist, agency and client to track changes in the client across the course of the therapy offered. Some other common assessment tools are the Beck Depression Inventory (BDI) and Beck Anxiety Inventory (BAI) (www.beckinstitute.org). The type of assessment may be unique to an agency and specifically designed to capture key information needed to ensure that a client is ready to undertake therapy, assess the impact of presenting material and measure risk (e.g. self-harm or suicidal ideation). In Chapter 2 we discussed the fact that different approaches to counselling and psychotherapy have different philosophical and theoretical underpinnings. This may have a direct impact upon assessments undertaken; for example, a psychodynamic therapist may be concerned to capture childhood history since relating in childhood is thought to influence later relationships. This (possibly additional) assessment may support you with any written work you need to undertake for your training provider, and this will be discussed later in the chapter. Assessment and review information may also be used by an agency to show the success of any therapeutic services they offer; for example, in bids to secure further funding for continuation of the service or in justification of the service to key stakeholders.

My placement is with a workplace counselling service. Although clients are free to bring any issue to counselling, the specific aims of the service mean that our assessment and outcomes are, in part, based specifically on the context. So when an assessment is done with a client, they will be asked whether they are currently at work or are off sick. This will also be recorded in the middle of the counselling (at review) and again when we end. The statistics from this suggest that the counselling service is successful in supporting people to return to work. Once a quarter, the service manager will present these numbers to the directors of the company as one of the ways to demonstrate how the service is benefiting the workforce and the company overall.

Record keeping

Once you have started work with a client, it will be necessary to make post-session notes. Again, with this component of your client work, convention will vary from organisation to organisation. At the very least, your agencies will require you to record dates of sessions attended or missed. In addition, you may be required to record key themes, progress or insight gained and details of issues such as risk assessment and/or ethical matters addressed.

> The Information Commissioner's Office provides a useful 'plain English' guide to data protection which is available online (see Information Commissioner, n.d.). This may help you define the obligations for both you and the agency you work within in terms of data protection.

Your agency may wish you to capture specific information in your notes in a particular way. Some notes may be kept on paper and stored securely by the agency. Some organisations may ask you to enter details into a secure database or online system. Whatever convention is adopted by your agency, notes will be made anonymous; that is, the client's name and any identifying details will not appear. This is usually achieved by way of a coding system, ensuring that no link can be made to the client other than by knowing the coding system used and cross-referencing the details. As well as acting as an aide-mémoire for the therapist, it is important to remember that your client has a right to access any information held about them under the Data Protection Act (1998).

Recording and writing about client work

As mentioned in Chapter 3, as part of your personal and professional development, and to support you in working towards qualification and/or professional accreditation/registration, it is likely that you will be audio-recording sessions with clients (where permissible). Recording and writing about client work creates a dual relationship (Gabriel, 2005) in that the therapist is using the relationship for more than one purpose (see Chapter 1 for further definition). As BACP (2013) suggest, dual relationships are rarely neutral and it is important to consider this carefully with your supervisor to ensure that work with your client continues to be based in ethical practice.

The specifics of recording will likely be explored during the initial assessment phase and followed up within the verbal and/or written contract. As mentioned previously, gaining informed consent is a complex and continuous matter for consideration with both client and supervisor. Some areas to address include:

- the nature of the notes/recordings including how they will be used (e.g. to support professional development in supervision or for review within the training context in support of qualification and/or professional accreditation/registration)
- how they will be stored and who will have access to them
- clients' 'rights', for example:
  - the right to stop the audio-recording at any time or decide they do not want a particular session to be recorded
  - the right to withdraw consent for recording or consent for recordings to be used in a particular way.

Your first client

At some point in this process you will be ready to start formal client work and you will receive your first referral. We recognise that this can be simultaneously daunting and exciting. This is an important landmark in your journey to qualification and professional recognition. Each trainee's response is going to be different to this significant event. It may be beneficial to reflect upon the thoughts and feelings evoked by the idea of seeing your very first client in order to identify and mitigate the effects of thoughts and feelings regardless of their nature. In order to do this, we invite you to undertake Activity 5.4 to examine your own responses to your very first session within placement.

Activity 5.4 Exploring the possible impact of the first session

Aim

- To enable exploration of responses to seeing your first client.

Background

At some point in this process you will be ready to start formal client work and you will receive your first referral. We recognise that this can be simultaneously daunting and exciting. This is an important landmark in your journey to qualification and professional recognition. Each trainee's response is going to be different to this significant event. It may be beneficial to reflect upon the thoughts and feelings evoked by the idea of seeing your very first client in order to identify and mitigate the effects of thoughts and feelings regardless of their nature.

Activity

- Think about your first session with a client; picture yourself in the room with the person you are about to see (if you have not yet received a referral it would be interesting to note how you picture your client).
- Make a note of any thoughts, feelings, images and so on that arise as you are reflecting on this event.
- Of these thoughts, feelings and images (etc.), note how any of these might:
  - support you in your first/ongoing sessions
  - hinder you in your first/ongoing sessions.
- Think about how you might harness potential positive impact and mitigate the effect of any potential adverse ones. Who can support you in exploring this?

A PDF version of this activity is available to download from https://study.sagepub.com/oldaleandcooke

Commencing Placement: Managing Practicalities, Processes and Relationships

You may wish to return to the above activity when you have seen your first few clients. Were your hopes realised and/or fears justified? How did you successfully manage your early client sessions?

The network of relationships

Once you start in placement, you immediately widen your network of professional relationships. Whilst you became part of the community of trainee therapists when you embarked on your training course, you are now also firmly at the centre of a network which includes your placement provider and colleagues, your supervisor and the wider network of professionals. This network is not, strictly speaking, hierarchical. That is, there is not any one person at the top of the hierarchy who has ultimate control of the psychotherapy and counselling professions. The network is internally self-supporting; it depends upon the integrity of the individuals within it and their collaboration with the ethical codes and frameworks of professional bodies. The training endeavour invests individuals with particular lines of responsibility. Training provider expectations with regard to these responsibilities were discussed when we introduced the notion of the three- and four-handed contract in Chapter 3. You may wish to return to Table 3.4 to re-familiarise yourself with these responsibilities as it will support you in developing understanding of key aspects of your placement in action.

Making the most of supervision

I was so pleased to secure a placement with both individual and group supervision available within the organisation. I've read something about the functions of supervision but I'm not sure how to use this effectively to support me in my training and with my client work in placement.

In Chapter 3 we introduced the idea of supervision, and how it might be used to support you in the process of preparing to start work with clients. We introduced Despenser's definition of supervision as 'a formal arrangement for therapists to discuss their work regularly with someone who is experienced in both therapy and supervision' (2011: 1). We considered how supervision practices may vary according to the therapeutic model and indicated the specific requirements stipulated within the three- and four-handed contracts underpinning and supporting the placement endeavour. Within this section, we wish to highlight the importance of making the most of your supervisory relationship and offer some pointers to support you to ensure that this is supportive to your work in placement and to your overall professional development.

You are most likely to benefit from supervision if you pay attention to a number of important factors, namely;

- **Contracting with your supervisor(s)** – this will include consideration of the initial working agreement as well as ongoing reviews of the relationship and process. Working in this way will no doubt support you in your understanding of what to expect from supervision and ensure that both your training and placement providers' requirements are attended to from the outset, together with making certain that your ongoing needs are attended to (initially as you begin placement and subsequently as a developing practitioner).
- **Preparing for each session** – it is vital to prepare for your supervision sessions. You might wish to use a specific framework in order to ensure a level of consistency and to support you to develop the discipline required for this. Although we include some examples later in this section, it is advisable to discuss this with your training provider and/or supervisor as they might have a preferred format.
- **Prioritising what to take to sessions** – we recommend consideration be given to how to use your time in supervision so that you can prioritise your needs and ensure that these are met. It will also be important to pay attention in this process to determine whether you are regularly leaving out certain clients and/or practice issues.
- **Identifying a clear starting point and focusing on process to avoid being content-driven** – for instance, it is essential that you and your supervisor develop a shared understanding of what brought the client to therapy in order to support ongoing work; however, the narrative (i.e. the story and how it is told – the intonation, expression, bodily expression, what was not said, etc.) can provide insight into the therapeutic process and relationship.

Using a set of subject areas (or questions) can provide a useful focus in support of supervision preparation, some examples might include:

- exploration of blocks in relationship with clients
- clarifying views, values, theoretical understanding
- exploring your understanding of the client's perspective
- consideration of different ways of responding
- looking at your use of self in relationship
- addressing ethical and professional issues (such as contracting)
- consideration of self-care; acknowledgement and exploration of stress; vicarious traumatisation; burnout
- identification, exploration and development of professional identity
- identifying further areas of professional development
- addressing organisational issues that are helping or hindering your work.

In addition, as indicated above, there are a number of things that you might usefully explore in supervision with regard to your early placement experience, for instance:

- the impact of early client work
- appropriate building of the client caseload
- discussion of important theoretical, ethical, developmental components of the work you are undertaking.

Commencing Placement: Managing Practicalities, Processes and Relationships

Impact of early client work

I recall vividly the time when I first started seeing clients. I often left sessions thinking, 'How will I ever be able to manage this?' and feeling as if I was deskilled or incompetent in some way or another. Although it seemed there was new learning to be gained every time I saw someone, my overriding feeling was worry! What I found particularly helpful when I went to supervision was to be able to explore what seemed like overwhelming responses and issues. With the help of my supervisor I was able to see I was sometimes working at the edge of my ability, trying to apply new skills and ways of relating. My supervisor said that feeling uncomfortable, deskilled and worried was inevitable – however, she suggested I try to see these responses in a more positive light ... that for my learning to progress I needed to practise, practise, practise and that in doing so I would develop and feel more satisfied about my work with clients! She was right! I have been able to use supervision to make clear plans of action, having untangled what belongs to clients and what was for me to take to personal therapy. I have been able to take aspects of this forward into my placement work – my confidence has increased and I noticed over time that I was less overwhelmed and more able to make sense of my experiences and identify that I have developed skills to help me decide what I need to do in client work and for myself!

The above illustrates something of the potential impact of commencing client work, highlighting how supervision plays an active role in supporting trainee therapists in their learning and professional development as they undertake the placement endeavour. It is important to remember that you are at the very early stages of acquiring a new skill set and it is likely that you will become acutely aware of your limitations or areas for development – sometimes at the expense of what you are doing well. Awareness of incompetence can provoke anxiety or a sense of being overwhelmed – a natural response to being outside your comfort zone when learning something new! One way to consider this aspect of your learning experience is via the conscious competence learning model (adapted from Burch's skill model (Gordon Training International, 2011)) which describes the following four stages involved in the process of progressing from incompetence to competence in a skill:

- *Unconscious incompetence* – you will be unaware of your own weaknesses or competence gaps.
- *Conscious incompetence* – you will be aware of your weaknesses or competence gaps but will not (yet) have overcome these.
- *Conscious competence* – you will be able to perform effectively in the area concerned but will need to make a conscious effort to do so.
- *Unconscious competence* – you will be able to perform effectively without any conscious or apparent effort.

If we apply this to the scenario at the beginning of this section, we could describe the trainee in question as somewhere between the levels of conscious incompetence and conscious competence. Initially, the person seems to be overwhelmed although aware of their limitations and inability to make sense of their experience (conscious incompetence). After active discussion with their supervisor, however, they identified a clear way forward both for the client and themselves, developing in confidence and being able to apply learning to future work (conscious competence). Rather than seeing this model as a set of static stages with the pinnacle at the unconscious competence stage, we would argue that the process is more fluid, with practitioners moving back and forth between the different stages according to a number of factors, including levels of client distress, client material and resonance to personal material and personal life circumstances.

The importance of monitoring the impact of client work when new to practice can ensure that at this early stage you are:

- working within your level of competence (which might be very different from being in a comfort zone, as the example above illustrates!)
- identifying any issues of personal and professional development early on and addressing these as appropriate (e.g. within the supervisory process or in personal therapy)
- ensuring that the impact of client work is not detrimental to your health and wellbeing, thus highlighting the importance of self-care and the BACP (2013) ethical principle of self-respect.

Also, this monitoring will play an important part in the process of deciding whether and when to increase and/or decrease client caseloads, ensuring ethical practice; this will be addressed in the next section.

Appropriately building the client caseload

It is likely that you will begin with a relatively low number of clients when you first start your placement. In part, this is to provide you with an opportunity to settle into work at a steady pace. How you build your client caseload will be dependent on a number of factors, but undoubtedly your supervisor can support you in this process. In your decision-making process, therefore, you might wish to consider:

- the impact of initial client work
- the potential impact of taking on further clients
- the time you have available
- any placement expectations about how many clients are seen
- your schedule for building towards the clinical total required by your training provider.

None of the above considerations overrides any of the others. Your wellbeing and the impact of the work you are undertaking must remain as a central consideration throughout practice, but particularly during training. Assessment information, if available, might be useful in supporting you to decide whether it is appropriate to work with a particular client. You may consider whether you are able to take on a client with particular issues, levels of distress or risk factors alongside the client caseload you have currently.

Do keep in mind that the size of your clinical caseload will impact your supervision requirements; your supervision hours will need to be proportionally in line with the number of client hours booked (see Chapter 3). This ensures that you maintain

Commencing Placement: Managing Practicalities, Processes and Relationships

the in-depth consideration of each therapeutic relationship throughout training. The impact of this upon time and financial resources might be another potential consideration in whether you are able to commit to additional client work. We would also stress here that the supervision ratios suggested are minimum levels, so you may wish to undertake further supervision should you feel it is necessary for any particular client relationship (e.g. you may find that working with a client with a high level of distress, or processes or material close to your own is more demanding).

Theoretical, ethical, developmental functions of supervision

In Chapter 2, we invited you to assess your readiness to practise by undertaking activities about your theoretical understanding, ethical understanding and your personal development. This will be an endeavour which is ongoing in supervision. Over and above the importance of these components to your development as a professional, it will likely be necessary to continually evidence your competence and fitness in each of these areas to both your training and placement providers so that your practice and continuation in training and placement can be endorsed.

Completing written work

Audio-recordings and records pertaining to your own process or learning in supervision will support you in the completion of the pieces of written work required by your training provider. You may find that as part of writing about your practice (e.g. within an essay, case study or a process report), your training provider asks you to evidence the key components we have discussed in this chapter, namely the processes of:

- referral
- assessment and review
- contracting
- record keeping.

Training providers will differ in regard to the amount of detail required in assessed written work, so do check with the information you have been given and clarify with your trainer if necessary.

Listening to and critiquing audio-recordings of your work and revisiting supervision-based notes will be of vital importance to your academic and professional success. Activity 5.5 lists some common aspects of the above processes you may be asked to write about in pieces of academic work (in particular, case studies or transcripts/process reports). We have provided space and made some suggestions as to what else you may need to consider and incorporate as a result of:

- the fact that the very act of recording and writing about your practice as part of the training endeavour impacts upon the relationship and may become part of the material discussed

- the requirements of pieces of work are likely to be individual to various training providers
- the resonances and dissonances between your core approach and the conventions of the agency in which you are undertaking placement.

Activity 5.5 Ways of utilising session material for professional development; practical and ethical considerations

Aim

- To facilitate exploration of the ways in which you might utilise session material for further development.

Background

As a trainee, you are required to evidence your learning and development via a variety of assessment processes, including in written work and when presenting aspects of client work in supervision. In addition, you will be expected to construct accurate records of key aspects of your professional practice by your placement provider.

Activity

Consider the following ways of capturing information from the therapeutic relationship:

- Referral information.
- Client assessments/reviews (including end of therapy assessments).
- Process/supervision notes.
- Recordings of sessions.

List some specific ways in which each of these can support you to:

- assess how you are settling into your placement
- develop personally and professionally in the placement context
- make the most of supervision
- support the written work completed for your training provider.

How will you ensure anonymity of client material in gathering and utilising the above?

Finally, consider how you might gain informed consent from your client/the placement for use of the material in some or all of the above ways:

- For instance, is this incorporated into the existing client contract for the agency? Will you need to create a separate contract for this purpose?
- What are the client and/or agency specific factors which may mean it is inappropriate to ask for informed consent, and why?

A PDF version of this activity is available to download from https://study.sagepub.com/oldaleandcooke

The following vignette offers insight into one trainee's reflections about the advantages of assessing in a variety of ways for both practise and academic work.

The agency I work for requests that I undertake three formal assessments based on the CORE system. I complete this with the client at the start, in the middle and at the end of therapy. The results from these give some invaluable information about risk, and are useful in showing shifts across the course of the work we are doing. As I have gained in experience I have come to see the CORE assessment as a useful way to help make sense of client incongruity – a concept central within my training course, which is primarily humanistic with emphasis on the person-centred approach. However, this assessment seems limited to me and so I choose to undertake an additional initial and ongoing assessment with each client. This involves me assessing the level to which my client and I can be in psychological contact with each other and how far the conditions of empathy and unconditional positive regard can be experienced and communicated by me and then are being perceived by my client. I also check out my responses to the client to assess how congruent or integrated I can be in the relationship. Doing this helps me to decide if I am working effectively with the client and allows me to take any doubts to supervision. There are some other advantages of working in this way too. I'm beginning to understand how theories work in practice and to test out whether these are useful. Also, I know that I have assessed the client in a way that is resonant with my training approach, and this will assist me when I come to write up case studies or include examples of my practice in my future essays.

Measuring success

Measuring your success and determining areas for development will be a continuous part of your reflexivity as a practitioner. Whilst in training, and particularly in the early stage of your placement, all of the stakeholders involved will be interested in how you are progressing. This will be undertaken in a number of diverse ways according to the needs and requirements of the stakeholders involved. What we have suggested here is a template through which you might engage with each party in the process, potentially over and above their official processes of assessment. They may support you in preparing for any formal assessments undertaken as these are likely to cover similar ground.

Earlier in the chapter, we mentioned four stages involved in the process of progressing from incompetence to competence in a skill. Undoubtedly, as you negotiate your way through early placement-based experience, you will be moving between the stages of unconscious incompetence, conscious incompetence, conscious competence and unconscious competence with great regularity. As we indicated earlier, this is a normal process. At some point, it is likely you will realise that you find yourself in the 'competence' categories more frequently. This marks the move from early to more established practice – a transition which has blurred boundaries, but through which all practitioners will inevitably journey.

The next chapter focuses on your advancing practice, including decisions you will be making as you continue in placement and eventually qualify as a counsellor or psychotherapist. The theme of reflexivity is maintained and we will present you with a number of areas to consider in your ongoing decision-making about your professional career and its direction(s).

Chapter summary and ongoing reflections

We hope that this chapter has given insight into some of the important considerations related to the commencement of placement, including initial preparation, induction processes and important ethical aspects of therapeutic work (such as assessment, contracting and review and the relevance of making effective use of supervision). We hope that this has contributed to your reflection and planning and that you feel prepared to commence work with clients as well as undertake the related areas of responsibility this brings as a trainee therapist in placement. If you have already taken these first steps, we hope that the chapter has provided some useful areas for ongoing reflection.

The following activity will support you to identify areas for ongoing reflection and work:

1. Record some initial thoughts and feelings as you come to the end of the chapter.
2. From these, identify one or two points which need expansion or further investigation. For example, you may have realised that despite already having been inducted into your agency there are areas requiring further clarification, or you may have identified aspects of your contract for audio-recording which need review; alternatively, you may now have some ideas about the ways in which you might make use of supervision in support of your early development.
3. Identify how you might initiate a discussion or gain the information you need in regard to the above.
4. Set yourself a realistic target to action your points for development or further discussion.

Further reading

For more information on record keeping, there is an interesting section about the consideration needed when a client asks to see their case notes in Peggy Dalton's chapter of *Hard-Learned Lessons from Counselling in Action* (Dryden, 1992). We would point once again here to the useful supervision text *Supervision in the Helping Professions* (Hawkins and Shohet, 2006). The legalities of working in the client context are covered in the BACP series Legal Resources for Counsellors and Psychotherapists (Sage). Of particular relevance to this chapter is *Confidentiality & Record Keeping in Counselling and Psychotherapy* by Tim Bond and Barbara Mitchels (2015). For those interested in advancing their knowledge regarding contracting process and the application of these to working in placement, we suggest *Integrative Counselling Skills in*

Action (Culley and Bond, 2011). Readers who are student members of BACP may find the *Making the Contract for Counselling and Psychotherapy* information sheet useful (Dale, 2010).

References

Beck Institute (n.d.) *Patient Assessment Tools.* Bala Cynwyd, PA: Beck Institute. Available at: www.beckinstitute.org/beck-inventory-and-scales/ (accessed 21.08.14).

Bond, T. and Mitchels, B. (2015) *Confidentiality & Record Keeping in Counselling and Psychotherapy*, 2nd edn. London: Sage.

British Association for Counselling and Psychotherapy (BACP) (2013) *Ethical Framework for Good Practice in Counselling and Psychotherapy.* London: BACP. Available at: www.bacp.co.uk/admin/structure/files/pdf/9479_ethical%20framework%20jan2013.pdf (accessed 23.3.14).

Core IMS (n.d.) *Outcome Measurement Tools.* Rugby: Core IMS. Available at: www.coreims.co.uk/About_Measurement_CORE_Tools.html (accessed 21.08.14).

Culley, S. and Bond, T. (2011) *Integrative Counselling Skills in Action.* London: Sage.

Dale, H. (2010) *Making the Contract for Counselling and Psychotherapy.* BACP Information Sheet P11. Lutterworth: BACP.

Despenser, S. (2011) *BACP Information Sheet S2: What is Supervision?* Lutterworth: BACP.

Dryden, W. (1992) *Hard-Learned Lessons from Counselling in Action.* London: Sage.

Feltham, C. and Dryden, W. (1993) *Dictionary of Counselling.* London: Whurr.

Gabriel, L. (2005) *Speaking the Unspeakable: The Ethics of Dual Relationships in Counselling and Psychotherapy.* Hove: Routledge.

Gordon Training Institute (GTI) (2011) *The Four Stages for Learning Any New Skill.* Solana Beach, CA: GTI. Available at: www.gordontraining.com/free-workplace-articles/learning-a-new-skill-is-easier-said-than-done (accessed 02. 02. 15).

Hawkins, P. and Shohet, R. (2006) *Supervision in the Helping Professions.* Maidenhead: McGraw-Hill Education.

HM Government (1998) *Data Protection Act.* London: Stationery Office.

HM Government (2010) *The Equality Act.* London: Stationery Office.

Information Commissioner (n.d.) *Guide to Data Protection.* Wilmslow: ICO. Available at: http://ico.org.uk/for_organisations/data_protection/~/media/documents/library/Data_Protection/Practical_application/the_guide_to_data_protection.pdf (accessed 21.08.14).

Mind (n.d.) *Who's Who in Mental Health.* London: Mind. Available at: www.mind.org.uk/information-support/guides-to-support-and-services/whos-who-in-mental-health/#.U_YX1cVdXSE (accessed 21.08.14).

Trevithick, P. (2005) *Social Work Skills: A Practice Handbook.* Buckingham: Open University Press.

Six

Placements in Perspective

This chapter will:

- Consider ways in which to reflect upon your professional development so far, including attention to the evaluation of the ongoing impact of placement work experience.
- Highlight some potential factors involved in deciding whether to continue gaining experience with your existing placement provider(s) and/or to seek out further placement opportunities.
- Discuss the importance of continuing professional development as well as continued use of supervision and personal therapy.
- Invite reflection in regard to the future of your career: qualification, professional registration and beyond.

As we closed the previous chapter we suggested that a time will come when you progress towards increased levels of conscious and unconscious competence as a therapist. This chapter works from the assumption that you have begun to accumulate experience of supervised work with clients within at least one placement setting. Having said this, we do think that reading this chapter can provide useful insight for those who have not yet reached this point in their professional development. It merely means that what is discussed may be much more future focused than present focused for you. It is useful to maintain some future focus whatever level of training and experience you have as a therapist.

Throughout the chapter we encourage reflexivity in regard to your personal and professional, theoretical and ethical learning as well as your client work experience within placement. With this in mind, we revisit each of these ideas to explore how experience gained so far has enhanced your understanding. Your ongoing use of supervision may well be part of the basis for this process and we discuss how you may continue to make best use of this professional relationship. Equally, when you qualify your relationship with your training provider will end, so we then turn our attention to future career development including consideration of registration/accreditation with a professional body and the necessity of continuing professional development.

This chapter will deliver a mixture of information and invitations to reflect. Where we invite you to reflect we have employed techniques from an approach called Appreciative Inquiry.

The assumptions underlying Appreciative Inquiry make it an invaluable tool to support your reflection upon placement experience(s). In brief, these assumptions are:

- *Something is* working within each situation in which we are involved.
- We create reality, and this reality can be seen and interpreted from a number of perspectives.
- When we choose to focus on something it becomes real.
- When we ask questions, outcomes are influenced.
- Although the future is unknown, we can carry forward our learning from past situations; in particular, those things that have worked well for us.

> Appreciative Inquiry is a tool used in numerous areas, including business and education. It allows positive reflection on what has gone before as a basis for planning for future potential (see Appreciative Inquiry Commons, n.d.).

(adapted from Barnes, 2007: 39)

We sincerely hope that your placement experience has proven to be both successful and rewarding. Appreciative Inquiry can equally be used to reflect on experience which has been difficult and/or challenging by focusing on what you have learned and how this influences your aspirations for the future. We suggest ways in which difficulties might be managed or how you might ethically end involvement with a placement provider should this be deemed the only viable course of action. This process of reflection would, of course, be undertaken in conjunction with your supervisor. Consequently, we consider how you might make best use of this professional relationship on an ongoing basis. Of course, trainees and qualified therapists decide to end or extend their relationships with placement organisations for a number of reasons, not all of which are problematic in their nature. These reasons (such as extending your clinical experience and gaining paid work as a therapist) are considered in this chapter also.

Our exploration commences with an activity based on Appreciative Inquiry, and we will continue to include points for reflection throughout the chapter to guide your reflections and planning.

Ongoing reflective practice

In Chapter 2 we defined reflexivity as 'action on reflection', citing Tosey and Gregory (2002: 138) who suggest that it is the fusion of being aware of our 'motivations, assumptions, thoughts and feelings' along with applying and acting on these in the world. Up until this point, your professional support network (e.g. your supervisor) has assisted you to settle into your placement and develop your capacity to manage the impact of working with clients. For instance, you most likely have considered 'motivations' in regard to the process of selecting an appropriate placement and addressed 'assumptions, thoughts and feelings' about settling into the organisation itself, including the clinical component. It is likely that these 'motivations, assumptions, thoughts and feelings' have transformed as a result of this reflection and that your capacity for reflexivity has developed and is becoming more sophisticated in nature.

Activity 6.1 invites you to consider appreciative questions about different aspects of the placement experience, including how these may have influenced your personal and professional development. It also invites you to make plans for the future. Do not worry if you do not feel ready to do this at this stage; the process of appreciative inquiry is organic and you may find yourself revisiting each area a number of times, utilising supervision and other areas of professional support to undertake its dialogic process. How and with whom you choose to undertake the activity is your personal choice. It is feasible that this type of reflection will continue throughout your professional career as a therapist. Later in this chapter, we discuss how this might form the basis for some important decisions about your ongoing career. Consequently, it would be useful to make a note of your ideas so that these are readily available to you as you read through the remaining chapter.

Activity 6.1 Applying appreciative questions to aspects of practice

Aim

- To use appreciative questions to enable reflection and goal setting in regard to various aspects of practice.

Background

Appreciative Inquiry is a tool used in numerous areas, including business and education. It allows positive reflection on what has gone before as a basis for planning for the potentiality of the future. The assumptions underlying Appreciative Inquiry make it an invaluable tool to support your reflection upon placement experience(s). In brief, these assumptions are:

- *Something is* working within each situation in which we are involved.
- We create reality, and this reality can be seen and interpreted from a number of perspectives.
- When we choose to focus on something it becomes real.
- When we ask questions, outcomes are influenced.
- Although the future is unknown, we can carry forward our learning from past situations; in particular those things that have worked well for us.

(adapted from Barnes, 2007: 39)

Activity

Reflect on the aspects of your placement suggested in Table 6.1 using the appreciative questions provided.

TABLE 6.1 Applying appreciative questions to aspects of practice

Define: Choose an area to focus on.	
For this area of focus explore: Themes and issues that arise when I reflect on: • What are the highlights? • What has gone well? • What have I learned from any challenges which have arisen?	
Dream/imagine: • How would you like it to be? • How do you envision your future in regard to this area?	
Design/delivery: • What specific steps will you take to move towards the future you envision? • How will you sustain this change? • How can existing/new support systems support you in these aims?	

(Continued)

(Continued)

- Professional development, including:
    - application of theory to practice
    - advancement of ethical understanding
    - use of therapeutic skills and attitudes
    - use of supervision.
- Relationship with placement organisation and people therein.
- Personal development.

A PDF version of this activity is available to download from https://study.sagepub.com/oldaleandcooke

How has client work impacted me?

If we take some time to reflect on the impact of client work, a number of areas of consideration might come to mind. You may remember that in Chapters 2 and 3 we invited pre-placement reflection in a number of areas:

- Motivations to work as a therapist and with particular client groups.
- Understanding and application of theoretical ideas from your core/integrative model.
- Understanding of ethics.
- Personal development.
- Therapeutic skills and attitudes.

Now that you have had experience of working within the placement context there is likely to have been a period of prolonged reflection on each of the above. The realities of working in a placement setting including experiences of client work and being confronted with ethical dilemmas will no doubt have challenged you both personally and professionally. Some of the theoretical ideas from your core training may have been evidenced through practice, whereas it is likely that other views will have been challenged and thrown into doubt. Potentially, there has been a change in the way that you view yourself and in your motivations to work as a therapist. Table 6.2 highlights a number of appreciative questions you might ask based on the experience you have accumulated in your client work so far.

Should I stay or should I go?

The responses and ideas you have charted in Activity 6.1 and following reflection on Table 6.2 may lead you to some decisions about whether (or not) you wish to continue in your placement post qualification. There may be a number of reasons why you or the organisation might end a placement, including:

- You wish to gain different experience, specialise with a different client group or in a different setting.

TABLE 6.2 Appreciative questions on key areas of experience

	How can my learning and development so far enhance my ongoing practice?			
Theory	Ethics	Therapeutic skills and attitudes	Personal development	Motivations to train/work as a therapist
How have theoretical ideas from my core training been supported/challenged by my experience of working in the therapeutic context? What have been some of the highlights in my insight/understanding? How does this enhance my ability to apply theory to practice? How do I describe my ongoing theoretical orientation?	What are the main learning points I have drawn from ethical decisions and dilemmas worked with thus far? How does this strengthen my ongoing understanding of ethics in practice? What does this mean for my ongoing work as an ethical practitioner?	How has the demonstration of my therapeutic skills and attitudes been enhanced by work with clients? How does my way of working complement the theoretical model I currently hold?	What have I learned about my Self and my Self-in-relationship with: • clients? • my placement organisation/colleagues? • my supervisor? • my training organisation? How will this learning enhance my ongoing professional relationships?	When I reflect on my original motivations to practise, how, if at all, has this been influenced by my actual work with clients? What are my current motivations for continuing to work with clients? What are my hopes for my ongoing career as a therapist?

- The placement has failed to secure further funding for a counselling service.
- The experience you hoped to gain within the placement has not come to fruition.
- The placement contract was time limited.
- You wish to gain paid employment as a therapist or start a private practice.
- Your personal circumstances have changed, making voluntary work no longer viable.

Equally, you might decide to commit to an organisation for a longer period of time. This might be due to the future opportunity of paid work if you complete a certain number of hours of practice, or the valuable experience and satisfaction you gain from working within a specific context. Alternatively, you may wish to continue in a voluntary capacity because you see benefits to working in the organisation over and above monetary ones, or for altruistic reasons.

Deciding to stay in placement

As a placement manager at a busy counselling service, I always appreciate those occasions when trainee therapists stay with us after they have qualified. We take this as a demonstration of the commitment of the individual concerned. In terms of our investment in them it means that we, as well as our clients, are able to gain from this on an ongoing basis. The fact that we have more experienced therapists on board means that we can offer support systems such as mentoring of newer trainees, making the new placement experience less daunting for them, and hopefully giving a rewarding further opportunity to qualified therapists.

After qualifying last year I decided to continue volunteering with my placement organisation. I felt committed to the organisation, to my colleagues and clients. I really valued the work of the organisation and could see benefit in continuing to work with a diverse client group. Although I had to reduce my time commitment due to securing part-time paid employment as a counsellor, I can see myself continuing to invest as a volunteer throughout my career – giving in this way fits with my personal value system!

If your relationship with the placement is going well, you may consider staying as a volunteer to gain further experience. Staying within placement is likely to be appreciated by the placement organisation and you may find that there are opportunities to diversify and build on the contribution you have already made by becoming involved in different ways.

Ending your relationship with a placement

In addition to the reasons we listed earlier, there may be further reasons why it is necessary to end your relationship with a placement. Counselling and psychotherapy training is inevitably demanding and you may find that a break from the commitments you have built up during this time is wise in terms of self-care. Monitoring your own fitness to remain practising is a key component of most ethical codes and frameworks. It is addressed by BACP in section 40 of their *Ethical Framework for Good Practice in Counselling and Psychotherapy*, which states that if a therapist's

> effectiveness becomes impaired for any reason, including health or personal circumstances, they should seek the advice of their supervisor, experienced colleagues or line manager and, if necessary, withdraw from practice until their fitness to practise returns. (BACP, 2013a)

This may be the case if you have had a particularly demanding client caseload (both in terms of numbers and severity of presenting issues), or you have been juggling a number of commitments to manage training.

Equally, some placements do not go on inevitably. Particularly in more volatile financial climates, some organisations may find funding for services withdrawn or reduced, meaning they need to close or make difficult decisions about feasible levels of staffing.

> The roots of the word 'sabbatical' come from the Hebrew word 'Shabbat' or Sabbath, a weekly day of rest, worship or reflection. The term 'sabbatical' is used traditionally in the helping professions to denote a period of time away from a usual role, to rest and recuperate, or undertake alternative activities.

In the above scenarios we are faced with the options of ending altogether with an organisation or taking a 'sabbatical'.

So from your responses to Activity 6.1 and Table 6.2, reflect on the appropriateness of the below scenarios given your current circumstances:

- continuing in your current placement to gain further experience
- taking on an additional counselling or psychotherapy role in a paid or voluntary capacity
- ending with your current placement and either:
    - gaining alternative experience in another paid or voluntary role, or
    - taking a break or sabbatical from client work.

Which of the above would be most life-enhancing for you right now? Which would best support your aspirations as a therapist? In the following sections we will consider the alternatives, discussing the implications of each in turn.

Ending with a placement has similar connotations to ending with a client. The process has personal, professional and ethical implications that warrant attention. You will know from your training and placement experience that ending is an important aspect of the counselling process. You may, by now, also have had experience of endings within your training group; for example, marking the occasion in some way. If we expand the idea of ending to the organisational level, there

> When considering a break or sabbatical from practice it is always advisable to contact your professional body, particularly if you are a registered/accredited member or hope to apply in the future. Most professional bodies have a time limit in which practitioners can accumulate countable hours following qualification. Equally, on taking a sabbatical for a prolonged period of time there may be criteria to meet in order to re-join your professional body as a full practising member.

are some parallels. Whilst working in placements, you will likely have engaged in relationships with numerous clients and staff members. You have formed an attachment with the organisation and for this reason the ending might be treated as the ending of a relationship. Therefore, when ending with a placement provider you will need to consider both practical and relational implications. Practical considerations may include:

- the notice period required by the organisation
- management of client endings, particularly for those requiring ongoing therapy
- ensuring client records are up to date.

Relational elements might include the impact of the ending:

- intrapersonally (i.e. on you)
- interpersonally (i.e. with clients and colleagues)
- organisationally overall.

These considerations might be discussed in supervision and/or via any case management processes used within your placement organisation. In terms of your personal process, Activity 6.2 might form a useful basis for reflection. The questions raised may also form useful points for consideration when reflecting on appropriate endings with clients.

Activity 6.2 Personal reflections on ending with a placement

Aim

- To facilitate consideration of the impact of ending with your placement provider with attention to personal and organisational processes.

Background

Ending with a placement organisation has similar connotations to ending with a client. The process has personal, professional and ethical implications that warrant attention.

Activity

Consider the forthcoming ending with your placement organisation, your colleagues and clients.

- What is your immediate response to this ending? Note thoughts, feelings and any images (etc.) which come to mind.
- How are these responses influenced by your experience of previous endings?

- In order to facilitate an ending which is satisfactory wherever possible for you, your colleagues and clients:
    - What personal processes do you need to reflect upon?
    - What organisational dynamics might you need to consider?
    - What client factors do you need to address and how might these interact with your own processes relating to ending?
- What discrete actions need to take place in order to facilitate a safe and ethical ending for you and the others involved in the process?

A PDF version of this activity is available to download from https://study.sagepub.com/oldaleandcooke

Securing further placement experience

If you decide to secure further placements in order to widen your clinical experience, your existing experience of search and recruitment processes can be drawn upon. It may be useful also to revisit Chapters 4 and 5 in order to familiarise yourself with ideas regarding search, application and interview processes and the initial stages of settling into a new placement. In addition, you now have the benefit of having reflected on your accumulating placement-based experience including client work to aid the application and interview process. This might incorporate attention to your theoretical knowledge, its translation into practice both with clients and in supervision; equally, you might consider ethical understanding and the range of dilemmas you have addressed within your work so far. You may decide to revisit some of the activities in Chapter 2; although these activities focused upon readiness, they might be used further to assess your initial and/or current motivations to practise generally and with particular client groups specifically. Reflecting on your personal and professional development will enable you to identify whether there are particular facets of potential new organisations or client groups required in order to facilitate your progress as a therapist.

My training course required only 250 hours of supervised client work as part of the qualification and I'm clear I want to gain accreditation as soon as possible so that I am in the best possible position to apply for paid work. It wasn't possible to stay on at my placement as it was a two-year fixed contract, so I've begun applying to other organisations. Completing the applications has enabled me to see how much I have gained over the past two years. I have lots of examples from my actual practice to include as evidence that I meet the job specification. I've also added concrete examples of ethical decisions I have made into my personal statement to emphasise my integrity and professionalism. Also, I've contacted a couple of organisations on the off-chance that they might be interested in keeping my details on file – one looks promising as they are keen to take on a couple of qualified volunteers to provide balance within their service, which is currently made up of beginning trainees only.

Ending your training and gaining qualification and professional recognition

Unless you are embarking on a further advanced training or are still in the process of accruing hours towards your qualification, any contracts you make from here on in will be context specific. These are likely to include a combination of you, the organisation(s) you work for, your supervisor and clients. The four-handed contracts which include your training organisation (discussed in Chapter 3) will now be obsolete. If you are continuing to work within the same placement context and with an existing supervisor we recommend that you re-contract, taking into account the fact you are now a qualified therapist. The placement organisation will likely have a three-handed contract for use in these instances to ensure clarity of responsibilitites of all those involved.

> As stressed in Chapter 3, all supervision hours suggested by professional organisations are a minimum. It is your responsibility as a practitioner to ensure that you are receiving sufficient supervision to meet your professional needs, including attention to your current client caseload. This may mean increasing hours when you have a demanding or increased caseload, or if, for example, specific personal issues are raised as a result of experiences within practice.

Other changes will also take place; for example, the requirement for the ratio between client hours and supervision will change from that required by your training/member organisation to at least the minimum required by your member organisation.

The experience of gaining your qualification can be seen as both an ending and a beginning. Alongside any formal graduation or celebration organised by your training organisation, there is the knowledge that the training group you have belonged to will not continue. Some relationships with colleagues and tutors may be enduring, others may end. New groups may be joined and along with this new relationships formed. The remainder of this chapter will focus on the future and aspects of the professional role of counsellor or psychotherapist you will need to consider as you embark on your career.

Professional membership

On qualification it is likely that the level of professional body membership you subscribe to will change from student to full member; this may require a letter or certificate from your training organisation as evidence. The organisation you are a member of may also have further levels of membership you might be eligible for or can work towards. For example, on gaining 450 hours of supervised face-to-face client work you are eligible to become:

- Registered with the British Association for Counselling and Psychotherapy (BACP), which involves completing a training course and if this course is not accredited by BACP, undertaking their certificate of proficiency.
- Accredited with the BACP, which involves completing the accreditation process.

- Registered with the United Kingdom Council for Psychotherapy, which is normally undertaken via a member organisation; that is, a training establishment through which you will gain your training and qualification hours.

Most professional organisations will ask members to evidence their continued practice and professional development both during the initial registration process and periodically thereafter in order to remain a member or to retain a particular level of membership. For this reason it is useful to continue to keep a log of client and supervision hours, as well as evidence of any continuing professional development undertaken. Ensuring this evidence base is up to date will ensure that you are prepared for any random audit processes which may be undertaken.

> For further specifics of criteria for the various levels of professional membership, please refer to individual professional bodies. Each will have their own requirements, which are likely to include minimum number of training hours, minimum ratio of client hours to supervision whilst training and minimum level of supervision thereafter. Other criteria may also need to be met and evidenced.

Finding paid work as a therapist

The hope of becoming a paid therapist may have been one of the main motivations for undertaking your therapeutic training. Whether full- or part-time, employment may be gained as a therapist on an employed or self-employed basis. Being a self-employed therapist can involve either working freelance for an organisation or setting up your own private practice. The information in Chapter 4 might equally be applicable to searching for paid work as a therapist if you wish to undertake this on an employed basis.

Employment

Employment as a counsellor or psychotherapist may occur in a number of contexts. Some of these contexts are discussed in more detail in Chapter 1. It may be that you wish to use placement experience gained with the particular client group in order to support an application for a similar role. You may be lucky enough to be offered a paid role within the placement organisation you have supported with your time and skills so far. Equally, you may decide to diversify and apply for a role in a different environment or with a different set of clients.

> I was thrilled when I was offered the chance to apply for a paid therapeutic role within the organisation for which I had volunteered since my second year of training. I had no hesitation in applying since I had been impressed from the outset with the set-up of the organisation, the support networks available and the opportunities provided to progress. Being given this opportunity really boosted my sense of value and confidence as a therapist and confirmed that applying to the organisation in the first place had been a prudent step.

I continued in my placement, for a year after I qualified, as a volunteer. By this time I was comfortable with the policies and processes and was pleased to offer support to newer incoming trainees. A sudden change in family financial circumstances, however, meant that I needed to consider paid work in the therapeutic field. Whilst I would have liked to have continued to volunteer some of my time indefinitely, I applied for various positions and was successful in gaining a position with a school counselling service. I really enjoy the new role, but always hope to return to volunteering my services as a therapist alongside this, at some point in the future, when finances allow.

The above vignettes show two different scenarios where qualified counsellors have decided to apply for paid work. Many therapists continue to volunteer alongside paid roles in either therapy or completely different areas. Whatever you decide, it is important that your decision suits you and your life circumstances, just as these practical considerations influenced your choice of initial placement provider.

Self-employment

> If you are planning on becoming self-employed in the United Kingdom, you can go to www.hmrc.gov.uk/. This website gives advice and guidance about registering as self-employed, your obligations with regard to completing an annual self-assessment and how to go about this. Some self-employed people do this individually, others decide to use an accountant to complete this important part of the process.

Some of the jobs advertised for therapists invite applications from those who are willing to join an organisation on a self-employed basis. This will usually mean that the company contracts to buy your services as a therapist at an agreed rate, rather than to take on the obligation of being your actual employer. Whether this is the case may depend on a number of reasons, including the size of the organisation and funding available to take on staff with employed status. Being self-employed within an organisation still means that when you join you will sign a contract and that you will be bound by their policies and procedures. You may even have access to benefits and continuing professional development offered within the organisation. However, you would in this scenario be responsible for paying your own tax and national insurance contributions, and would need to register with HM Revenue and Customs as self-employed in order to do so (see HMRC, n.d.).

Private practice

Being in private practice is again a form of self-employment, therefore the above details with regard to registering with HMRC, tax and national insurance apply. In this scenario, however, you would be responsible for sourcing clients to work with rather than gaining referrals through a single dedicated organisation. You may decide to advertise by various means, including a website, business cards, networking, posters and so on. It is important to consider professional body guidelines about how services are advertised. Great care must also be taken when describing what you do to ensure that this is accurate and provides potential clients with clear indication about how you work so they can make an informed decision about making initial contact with you. As an alternative or in addition to advertising, you may decide to accept referrals from an organisation such as an Employee Assistance Programme (EAP).

Since the private practice is your own business you will need to decide where you are going to undertake this work, and ensure that the premises are appropriate and safe (for both therapist and client). Working from home is an option selected by some therapists, although personal safety needs to be considered carefully in this instance – especially if you are likely to be alone when clients are seen. For some therapists isolation is lessened by working in premises specifically set up for counselling or other therapeutic purposes or in offices which can be converted for purpose. If you do decide to work from home you will need to inform your home insurer that this is occurring, and in some cases this may have an impact on your insurance premium. If you have a family you will need to think carefully about where in the home to base your work and how the space can be successfully managed between those who share it. Other considerations such as how pets are managed in the time you are working and whether the space is made neutral (i.e. free of family photographs, etc.) are important.

> A full list of EAPs registering with the Employee Assistance Professionals Organisation can be found at www.eapa.org.uk/. Contact each organisation individually to discuss their individual recruitment processes and whether registration/accreditation with a professional body is required.

Some further points for consideration before setting up private practice are:

- the necessity to write your own contracts outlining key points including fees, frequency of meeting, cancellation policies, limits to confidentiality and so on
- defining assessment, review and ending and referral processes
- determining what level of fees need to be charged in order to gain an appropriate income given possible outgoings (including renting premises, supervision, professional liability insurance)
- deciding how you will keep notes and information about clients safe and secure in line with the Data Protection Act.

> When I qualified as a therapist I decided to continue as a volunteer at the hostel where I had been working. However, it had always been my aim to set up a private practice so I decided to do this alongside my current volunteering commitments. After costing up suitable rooms in the locality and thoroughly considering the ethical and safety aspects of working from home with my supervisor I decided that renting rooms was not financially viable if I was to make any kind of income from the endeavour.

> The Information Commissioner's Office (ICO, http://ico.org.uk/) can help you to decide whether you need to register as a data controller. If you are keeping client records in a computerised format, this will be the case for you. The website has a useful online test which can help you to determine your obligations.

I decided to convert our spare bedroom into a therapy room, whereas previously it had always been used as a study (and dumping ground!). The cost of converting the room was minimal, a lick of paint, some seating and neutral pictures for the walls. The arrangement works really well as long as I keep my partner informed of what appointments I have day to day. I am not sure how thrilled my other half is about keeping quiet at times when I have clients, and the cat sometimes manages to sneak in under the sofa. I'm also a bit more obsessive about keeping the bathroom clean and tidy – just in case a client needs to go and pay a visit!

Continuing professional development (CPD)

Once qualified in any profession it is common good practice to keep up to date in your field of expertise using a variety of methods.

A number of activities might be defined as CPD with the emphasis on the proviso that participation in the endeavour contributes to your professional development and supports your ongoing competence as a therapist. These might include:

- ongoing supervision and personal therapy
- attending and/or delivering training courses and workshops
- being a delegate at and/or presenting at conferences
- research and writing activities
- reading books, papers, articles
- book reviewing.

BACP (2013b) cites the Professional Associations Research Network (PARN), which defines CPD as 'any process or activity that provides added value to the capability of the professional through the increase in knowledge, skills and personal qualities necessary for the appropriate execution of professional and technical duties, often termed competence.'

Some qualified (and indeed trainee) therapists decide to set up CPD groups. There are clear advantages in getting together with a group of colleagues, which can enhance development. Groups may decide on an agenda of topics of interest to the group, allocate speakers or facilitators on a rolling basis, or discuss a book each person agrees to read. In addition, CPD groups can form an important connection with other professionals in what can sometimes be an isolating role. If therapists are from different modalities, healthy cross-theoretical dialogue is encouraged between a diverse range of professionals. Do not rule out activities which might not at first glance be seen as CPD; the following therapist gives an example.

I noticed as I was looking through the local press that there was an exhibition at a local art gallery created by Holocaust Survivors. I decided to go along and the experience was thoroughly moving and traumatic at times. On discussion with my supervisor I have decided to record this activity as CPD – it helped me to reflect on the nature of prejudice and power in society and has undoubtedly enhanced my perspective, and hopefully my practice as a result.

TABLE 6.3　Continuing professional development activity log

Date	Activity undertaken	Number of hours	Personal and professional reflections

Whatever form of CPD activity undertaken, it is useful to keep an up to date log with any certificates you may accumulate. We have suggested a format for this log in Table 6.3. This includes space to record the date and type of activity and the number of hours undertaken as well as your own reflections. This section is included because maintaining registration/accreditation with a professional body requires you to provide explicit evidence of continuing competence and what you have gained from the CPD activity in terms of your professional practice. We hope that this proves a useful tool or gives you ideas for how you may record CPD in your own way.

Ongoing supervision

We mentioned above that supervision is an essential part of the CPD portfolio of a professional therapist and your member organisation will inform you of the minimum levels deemed to promote ongoing competence. Additionally, you will be developing what Casement (1985) calls an 'internal supervisor'. The idea is that the therapist becomes more independently able to undertake the kind of reflection which would have been facilitated by the supervisor in earlier practice. This ability to reflect means that the therapist is developing independence in practice and may find that what they discuss in supervision changes in focus or intensity. They might find themselves reflecting on their own 'internal supervisory' reflections and gaining feedback on these themselves from their supervisor. Therefore, as the qualified therapist gains independence and confidence in practice, their relationship with their supervisor may change. We would stress the importance here of continued supervision throughout the professional career as not only a professional responsibility but as an opportunity to reflect with another who may be able to offer alternative perspectives. This will increase the potential, for example, to identify blind spots in practice, process, repeated patterns and ensure the increased safety of both therapist and client. Figure 6.1, which originally appeared in Chapter 3, reminds us that supervision has multiple functions and some overlaps with personal therapy.

The next section will discuss those cases when you might decide to return to or continue personal therapy to support your ongoing development as a therapist.

Ongoing personal therapy and its alternatives

Sometimes supervisory support or other reflection can identify previously unknown issues or recurring themes which warrant unpacking in more detail. At this point, you may decide to use personal therapy as an alternative means of support as a person and a practitioner. You may return to a therapist you have worked with in the past or decide to seek a new therapist. Of course, personal therapy is only one way to work through something which may be affecting you personally and/or professionally. Other life-enhancing activities where you have the opportunity to explore in safety your thoughts and feelings, or discharge some of the demands of being a therapist (and many other roles simultaneously) may be more suitable for you as an individual; equally, this might be in addition to returning to therapy. The following examples illustrate this.

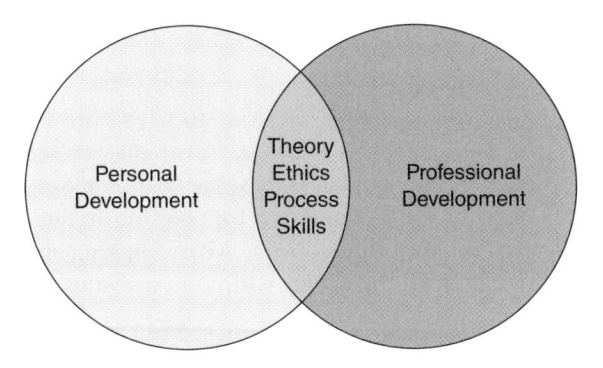

FIGURE 6.1 *Function of supervision*

Another member of my supervision group sensitively fed back to me during a session that I had persistently avoided one of the avenues my client was suggesting they might like to explore. This acted a little like a light bulb going on in my head, and I found myself making links to previous life experiences and also avoidance of other situations in my day-to-day life. For this reason I decided to return to personal therapy and so far this has been an invaluable experience. I can see my avoidance clearly as well as the reasons behind it and I am more able to support my client with my renewed personal awareness.

I had noted in supervision that I had increasing difficulty in 'switching off' after a day with clients. After a thorough exploration of whether this was hooked to client material and my own responses, I decided that the problem was more practical. I simply was not allowing myself enough time to wind down after a day of work. As a result I decided to attend a yoga class straight from work, which I have found hugely beneficial in defining the space between my time and my client time. It has connected me with a sense of calm which I didn't experience previously, and I am sure that I will continue to practise yoga throughout my life.

Ongoing assessment of competence

During your therapeutic training, your competence was assessed in a number of ways by your training provider. This may have involved writing essays, case studies or process reports as well as demonstrating your skills within group activities. Your supervisor and placement provider may also have been invited to validate your progress in some way; for instance, by providing annual written reports. Although you will continue supervision throughout your professional career, you will hold the primary responsibility for assessing the efficacy of your practice and monitoring the levels of your fitness and competence. Some organisations may provide tools with which to assess client progress throughout the therapeutic relationship; however, honest personal reflection on your practice is consistently necessary. We gave you an example earlier of an extract from the BACP ethical framework citing each individual practitioner's responsibility to evaluate their ongoing fitness to practise. One way to undertake this assessment might be to consistently revisit the core ways in which we initially invited you to assess your readiness to commence placement:

- theoretical understanding
- ethical understanding
- therapeutic skills and attitudes
- personal/professional development.

In this chapter you have already undertaken some of this reflection in respect of assessing appropriate steps for you to undertake for your future career. There are some other factors which may be taken into account when thinking about whether what you do works (in particular, with the clients with whom you work):

- Valuable information can be gained from your clients through assessment, review and ending processes, all of which you can reflect upon in supervision. This can provide evidence to determine whether or not you are working effectively in promoting change and understanding.
- Some therapists continue to or periodically audio-record work with clients in order to undertake more in detail reflection on sessions within supervision.
- Some of the CPD activities previously suggested might support you in understanding developments in the field, including new and innovative techniques.
- Engaging with research can support you to develop aspects of your professional identity:
  - Undertaking research means you can develop your own area of expertise and support the psychotherapeutic profession in demonstrating what works, whether through qualitative or quantitative studies.
  - Being an active consumer of research, whether through reading research articles or meta-analyses of research studies, can support you in justifying the efficacy and ethical soundness of your own approach to therapy.

We are certain that you have many other ways in which you ensure that your ongoing practice as a therapist is safe, effective and ethically sound.

Chapter summary and further reflections

This chapter has considered the importance of sustaining your ongoing reflections in regard to your professional career as a therapist using appreciative inquiry at the outset to demonstrate one method of supporting this. We have included consideration of decisions about whether or not you remain in your relationships with a particular placement provider. In addition, we have explored ongoing professional responsibilities including the potential of setting up a private practice, gaining a paid role as a therapist, and the professional responsibilities that go along with each. As you reflect on your ongoing development, consider:

1. What has been striking about this chapter? What are your thoughts and feelings in response to the points raised?
2. Which points for reflection do you feel need further consideration? For example, you may wish to think more about setting up private practice or gaining paid or voluntary experience in another context.

3. Set some specific learning objectives in relation to the above; for example, you may decide to do an in-depth job search for paid therapy roles using some of the information given in Chapter 4, or you may wish to investigate agencies that take on qualified volunteers.
4. Set yourself a timeframe in which to complete the above.

Further reading

For further insight into how Appreciative Inquiry might be applied in the therapeutic setting, in particular within supervision, there is an interesting and accessible chapter by Julie Barnes in Tudor and Worrall's (2007) edited text *Freedom to Practise (Volume II)*, entitled 'Using Appreciative Inquiry in Person-Centred Supervision'. The website Appreciative Inquiry Commons (http://appreciativeinquiry.case.edu/) contains a number of interesting articles on the applications of the approach in various settings. Tim Bond and Barbara Mitchels' book *Confidentiality & Record Keeping in Counselling and Psychotherapy* (2015) could prove useful if you are planning to start a private practice. If you are a member of BACP you can access their information sheets on various practical elements which would be useful in starting your own practice, including contracting, note keeping, confidentiality and setting up a therapy room.

References

Appreciative Inquiry Commons (n.d.) *What is Appreciative Inquiry?* Cleveland, OH: Weatherhead School of Management. Available at: http://appreciativeinquiry.case.edu/intro/whatisai.cfm (accessed 14.05.13).
Barnes, J. (2007) 'Using Appreciative Inquiry in Person-Centred Supervision', in K. Tudor and M. Worrall (eds), *Freedom to Practise, Volume II: Developing Person-Centred Approaches to Supervision*. Ross-on-Wye: PCCS Books. pp. 37–56.
Bond, T. and Mitchels, B. (2015) *Confidentiality & Record Keeping in Counselling and Psychotherapy*, 2nd edn. London: Sage.
British Association for Counselling and Psychotherapy (BACP) (2013a) *Ethical Framework for Good Practice in Counselling and Psychotherapy*. London: BACP. Available at: www.bacp.co.uk/admin/structure/files/pdf/9479_ethical%20framework%20jan2013.pdf (accessed 14.05.13).
British Association for Counselling and Psychotherapy (BACP) (2013b) *CPD*. London: BACP. Available at: www.bacp.co.uk/cpd/index.php (accessed 28.05.13).
Casement, P. (1985) *On Learning from the Patient*. London: Tavistock/Routledge.
Cheetham, G. and Chivers, G.E. (2005) *Professions, Competence and Informal Learning*. Cheltenham: Edward Elgar.
Employee Assistance Provider Association (n.d.) *Find an EAP Provider*. Derby: EAP Association. Available at: www.eapa.org.uk/ (accessed 21.08.14).

HMRC (n.d.) *Self-Employed*. London: HMRC. Available at: www.hmrc.gov.uk/self-employed/ (accessed 21.08.14).

Information Commissioner (n.d.) *Data Protection Registration: Self-Assessment*. Wilmslow: ICO. Available at: http://ico.org.uk/for_organisations/data_protection/registration/self-assessment (accessed 21.08.14).

Tosey, P. and Gregory, J. (2002) *Dictionary of Personal Development*. London: Whurr.

Index

ABCDE model, 59, 61, 66
academic work required from prospective therapists, 53, 70, 139
accreditation, 41, 52–3, 67, 69, 154, 160
acknowledgement of feedback, 65
advertising of counselling and psychotherapy services, 156–7
anxiety
   from awareness of incompetence, 137
   in response to assessment, 58–9, 62, 64
application forms, 92–3
applying for a placement, 89–98
   deciding where to apply, 89–92
   process of, 92–3
   speculative approaches, 98
   writing a personal statement, 93–7
appreciative inquiry, 144–6, 162
appreciative questions, 146–9
aptitude as a therapist, components of, 41–2
Asay, T.P., 33, 39
assessment
   of clients, 120, 126, 132
   of therapists, 58–62, 114, 161–2
assumptions about clients, 128–30
asylums, 9
audio-recording of sessions with clients, 133, 139, 162

Bager-Charleson, S., 26–7
Beck Depression Inventory (BDI) and Beck Anxiety Inventory (BAI), 132
behaviourism, 12
Bond, T., 11
Branch, R., 106
British Association for Counselling and Psychotherapy (BACP), 7, 17, 41, 45, 52, 67–8, 78, 88, 133, 151, 154, 158, 161
   principles upheld by, 29, 138
British Psychological Society (BPS), 67
buildings worked in by therapists, 123–4, 157
business cards, 89

candidate group interviews, 99
Casement, P., 160
Certificate of Proficiency (BACP), 67
client caseloads, 138–9

client involvement in feedback, 64
client non-attendance, 69
Clinical Outcomes Routine Evaluation (CORE), 132
cognitive behavioural therapy (CBT), 12
competence, 30–1, 24–5, 40, 52–3, 58, 67, 158
   conscious and *unconscious*, 137–8, 141, 144
   definition of, 24
   evidence of, 139
   levels of, 130, 137–8
   limits to, 25
   ongoing assessment of, 161–2
confidentiality, 79
   breaches of and limits to, 79
   policies on, 17
'conscious competence' learning model, 137–8, 141
continuing professional development (CPD), 158–62
   definition of, 158
contracting
   definition of, 74
   to provide services for an organisation, 156
   with a supervisor, 136
contracts, therapeutic, 4, 74–5, 120, 126, 131–2, 154, 157
   three- and *four-handed*, 75–6, 135, 154
'counselling', use of the term, 11
counselling and psychotherapy
   different modalities in *see* modalities
   as a distinct professional realm, 12
   historical background, 8–11
   organisational settings for, 12–14
'counsellor', use of the term, 89
curriculum vitae (CV), 92, 96–7

data protection and Data Protection Act (1998), 79, 128, 133, 157
decision-making processes, 30–1, 51, 138
deontological approach to ethics, 37
Despenser, S., 71, 135
disability, disclosure about, 85
disclosure by applicants, 85
Disclosure and Barring Service (DBS), 108
distress of clients, 8, 77
Dryden, W., 32, 39, 127
dual relationships, 17, 133
duty of care, 77

eclectic therapeutic practice, 12, 32
electronic media, use of, 86–7
Ellis, Albert, 12, 59, 66
employee assistance programmes (EAPs), 157
employment in counselling or psychotherapy, 155–6
ending a placement, 148–53; possible reasons for, 148–50
Equality and Human Rights Act (2010), 85, 124
'errors in thinking', 106–7
ethical awareness, 36–9
ethical codes and frameworks, 7, 25, 37, 39, 52, 77–8, 114, 128, 135
ethical stance, 25–6
ethical thinking as a process, 38
experience gained in placement, 5–7
external influences on organisations, 17

family relationships, 9, 44, 157
feedback
    on applications, 99
    client involvement in, 64
    on interviews, 108–9
    learning from, 66
    from observers and the observed, 62–4
    from supervisors, 160
    supporting the search/application process, 66–7
    use of, 64–6
fees charged by therapists in private practice, 157
Feltham, C., 32, 127
'fight or flight' response, 105–6
first session with a client, 134–5
fitness to practice, 24, 28, 30–1, 40, 58, 67, 150–1
    definition of, 24
    evidence of, 139
    monitoring of, 161
freelance working as a therapist, 155
Freud, Sigmund, 11–12
funding, allocation of, 15–16
'future focus', 144

Gregory, J., 25, 145
group interviews, 99–100
groups for continuing professional development, 158
The Guardian, 88

Hawkins, P., 72
health professions and organisations, glossary of, 125
health and safety issues, 122, 124
Hippocrates, 8
home of the client, services provided in, 124
home of the theapist, working from, 157
hours of work required for qualification and accreditation, 67–70, 85, 126, 154

implementation of objectives, 65
independence in therapeutic practice, 160

induction, 113, 119–26
    getting to know the organisation and its building, 119, 121–5
    into therapeutic practice, 119–21, 126
Information Commissioner's Office, 133, 157
informed consent, 71, 79, 133
insurance, 78
integration of placements within a programme of study, 5
integrative therapy, 12, 32
interacting in a group setting, 99–100
'internal supervisor', 160
interpreters, use of, 16
interviews for placements, 39, 98–109
    feedback on, 108–9
    possible questions, 103–5
    practical tips for the day itself, 106–8
    practice-based, 100

Jenkins, P., 77
job descriptions, 92
job fairs, 86–7

Kent, R., 77
Kolb, D.A., 33, 80
Kraepelin, Emil, 9

Lambert, M.J., 33, 39
learning cycle, 33, 48, 80
learning models, 137–8
learning objectives, 79–80, 111
Libya, 18
local group events, 86
lone-working policies, 124

McLeod, J., 7, 11, 32, 39, 41
malpractice claims, 78
'mastery of technique' (McLeod), 41
material resources affecting placements, 15
Mearns, D., 1, 42
medical conditions, disclosure of, 85
membership organisations, 151, 155
Mind (charity), 125
modalities in counselling and psychotherapy, 11–12, 31–2, 37, 70–1
    differences between, 25
    cross-theoretical dialogue between, 158
module-based placements, 5
motivations to become a therapist, 26–30, 148
    working with a particular group or area of concern, 28–30
multi-agency working, 125
multidisciplinary environments, 6

negligence claims, 78
networking, 86, 135
newspapers, 88

objectives, 64–6; *see also* learning objectives
observation, 3, 62–4
online forums, 86
organisational resources and structures, 16–17
organisational settings, 19–20
outcomes from therapy, determinants of, 33–4

paid work as a therapist, 150, 155–6
panel group interviews, 99
peers, information from, 86
the people the working in the placement organisation, 125
person-centred values, 12
person specifications, 92–3
personal development of the therapist, 39–48, 54, 138, 153
'personal soundness', 39–40
personal statements in placement applications, 93–7
personal therapy for therapists *see* therapy for therapists
philosophy, definition of, 31
placement
  benefits to be gained from, 45
  in counselling and psychotherapy as distinct from other helping professions, 3–5
  definition of, 1, 3
  as distinct from counselling and psychotherapy itself, 11–14
  environmental influences on, 14
  features looked for by trainees, 83–4
  features looked for by training providers, 85–6
  internal influences on, 15
  practical limitations on, 45–6
  role and purpose of, 4–5
  searching for, 24–6, 82, 86
  setting up your own, 109–10
  staying on to gain more experience in, 150, 153
  types of experience offered by, 5–7
placement fairs, 86
placement providers, 11, 14–20
  features looked for in applications, 99
  features looked for in presentations, 102–3
  feedback from, 99
  information from, 85
  information on, 89
  requirements of, 139
  responsibilities of, 4
planning 66, 146
  ability needed by therapists, 116
  reflective and *checklist* approaches to, 116
pluralistic perspectives on therapy, 12
policies, definition of, 16
post-qualification placements, 5
practical considerations affecting placements, 45–6, 58, 116, 152
practice-based interviews, 100
practice-based requirements, 53–4

premises used for therapy, 15, 123–4, 157
presentations, 100–8
  what placement providers look for in, 102–3
presenting oneself, 105
prior experience, 41
private practice as a therapist, 155–8
private sector organisations, 13
procedures, definition of, 16
Professional Associations Research Network (PARN), 158
professional bodies, 5, 7, 41, 51–2, 78, 88, 154–7
  guidelines from, 73, 157
  membership of, 154
professional considerations, 75–9, 119
professional development, 5–6, 40, 138, 153–6
  reflection on, 42–3
  see also continuing professional development
professional indemnity insurance, 78
psychiatry, 9, 11
psychoanalysis, 11
  training in, 25
psychodynamic therapists, 132
psychopharmacology, 9
'psychotherapist', use of the term, 89
The Psychotherapist (periodical), 88
public liability insurance, 78
public sector organisations, 13

qualifications in counselling and psychotherapy, 53

'rational' belief systems, 59
rational emotional behavioural therapy, 59
readiness of the client for therapy, 132
readiness to practice, 30–2, 34, 38–42, 44, 48, 51–8, 66–7, 78, 93, 139
  assessment of, 54–7
record-keeping, 70–1, 89–92, 111, 120, 133, 139, 155–60
referees, 98
referrals, 120, 125–30
  definition of, 127
  information included in, 128
  onward, 130
  receipt of, 127–8
reflection, 29–31, 51, 65–7, 111, 145–6, 160
  on ethical awareness, 36–9
  on personal and professional development, 39–48, 153
  on philosophical and theoretical understanding, 31–6
  pre-placement, 29, 33, 37, 48, 148
  from *reductionist* and *holistic* perspectives, 42
  on therapeutic practice and skills, 41, 161–2
  see also self-reflection
reflective practice, 145–8
reflexivity, 141, 144, 146
  definition of, 25

research, engagement with, 162
reviews of therapy, 121, 126
risk, 132
Rogers, Carl, 11–12
role play, 64

sabbaticals, 151
safety
    for the client and the therapist, 77–8, 157
    financial, 78
    see also health and safety issues
school counsellors, 127
search terms, 87
self, theory of, 32
self-assessment, preparing for, 57–8
self-care for therapists, 138, 150
self-employed therapists, 155–6
self-presentation and 'self-sabotage', 105–6
self-referrals, 126–7
self-reflection, 26
Shohet, R., 72
Shorter, E., 9
significance of a placement
    for the placement provider, 7
    for the profession, 7
    for the trainee, 6
    for the training organisation, 6
skill in the therapeutic context, definition of, 41
SMART objectives, 64–6
social gatherings, 86
specialised services in counselling and psychotherapy, 28–9
staff systems, 17
stakeholders in placements, responsibilities of, 4
standard-setting, 7, 52
success, measurement of, 141–2
supernatural causes of mental problems, 8
supervision, 40, 45, 51, 67, 68–74, 77, 135–9, 154, 160–2
    definition of, 71, 135
    functions of, 72, 139, 160–1
    models of, 72
    as an opportunity for reflection, 162
    preparing for sessions of, 136
    pre-placement use of, 73–4
    prioritisation and focusing in, 136
    requirements for, 85
    responsibilities of supervisors, 5

supervision *cont.*
    selection of supervisors, 73
    throughout a professional career, 160–1
    time needed in relation to client hours, 69, 138–9, 154
Sussman, M.B., 26–7

taxation, 156
theoretical understanding, 31–3
theory, 31–2
    definition of, 31
    metaphors for, 32
    of self and *of therapy*, 32
therapeutic process, 126
therapeutic relationship, 33
therapy for therapists, 40, 77
    alternatives to, 160–1
    ongoing, 160
Therapy Today (periodical), 88
Thorne, B., 39
Tosey, P., 25, 145
trainees, responsibilities of, 4
training providers, 4–5, 31
    guidelines from, 73
    information from, 86
    requirememts of, 52–71, 74–5, 78, 114, 139–40
    responsibilities of, 4
transpersonal therapies, 12
Trevithick, P., 116

UK Association of Humanistic Psychology Practitioners (UKAHPP), 31
understanding
    of ethics, 37
    philosophical and *theoretical*, 31–5
United Kingdom Council for Psychotherapy (UKCP), 7, 52, 67–8, 78, 88, 155
unpaid nature of placements, 1–4, 7
utilitarian approach to ethics, 37

validation of progress as a therapist, 161
voluntary sector, features of, 13
volunteering, 3, 150, 156

websites as sources of information, 87
Wilson, R., 106
word of mouth, seeking information by, 86
writing about therapeutic practice, 114, 132–3, 139–40